GUITAR *signature licks*

W9-BXS-600

best of George **Benson**

by Wolf Marshall

Cover Photo by Caroline Greyshock

ISBN 0-634-01131-6

HAL•LEONARD®
CORPORATION

7777 W. BLUEMOUND RD. P.O. BOX 13819 MILWAUKEE, WI 53213

Visit Hal Leonard Online at
www.halleonard.com

INTRODUCTION

Jazz guitar virtuoso, international pop superstar, fusion pioneer…George Benson has done it all. Originally inspired by Charlie Christian, Benson paid his dues in the rough-and-tumble bar circuit of Pittsburgh and environs. He was leading and fronting an R&B combo before Brother Jack McDuff hired him for his hard-bop organ group in 1962. Benson received his jazz apprenticeship on the road with McDuff and emerged as the genre's most important guitarist since Wes Montgomery. Benson's credentials were established with a series of albums as a leader on Prestige, Columbia, and Verve. He broke more new ground during his early 1970s CTI period and achieved pop stardom in 1976 with his first Warner Brothers record, *Breezin'*. The rest is history. Commercial successes aside, Benson's significance as a musician cannot be overstated. Like his forebears and fellow innovators, Wes Montgomery and Charlie Christian, Benson raised the art of jazz guitar to a new level and formed the next link in the chain of the instrument's evolution. The compositions and improvisations in this volume chronicle that remarkable musical sojourn with a detailed look at George Benson's style through the various epochs.

Enjoy,

—Wolf Marshall

THE RECORDING

Wolf Marshall: guitars (and bass guitar on "Body Talk")
Mike Sandberg: drums and percussion
John Nau: keyboards
Fred Kaplan: organ on "So What"
Denny Croy: bass
Connie Ruber: saxophone

Recorded at Pacifica Studios and Marshall Arts Music Studios.
Produced by Wolf Marshall.

Wolf Marshall plays archtop guitars by Gibson USA, and Fender Twin Reverb and Deluxe Reverb amps by Fender Music Instruments. The guitar parts on this recording were played using Thomastik-Infeld George Benson GB114 and Swing Series JS 113 flatwound strings.

Special thanks to Henry Johnson for his insights into the George Benson style.

For more on jazz guitar and the music in this volume, please visit *Wolf Marshall's Guitarland* at http://www.wolfmarshall.com on the worldwide web.

All selections transcribed by Wolf Marshall.

EASY LIVING
Theme from the Paramount Picture EASY LIVING
(The New Boss Guitar of George Benson, 1964)
Words and Music by Leo Robin and Ralph Rainger

Figure 1—Intro and Head

"Easy Living" was a leading track from George Benson's debut recording. Many jazz artists have made this venerable standard a part of their repertory, including vocalist Billie Holiday, trumpeter Clifford Brown, pianist Bill Evans, and guitarist Johnny Smith (an early influence on Benson). Benson plays the tune as a slow ballad in the original key of F with a traditional jazz guitar chord-melody style, employing a light, strummed articulation throughout. He casts the arrangement of the head and intro in a trio setting: guitar, bass, and drums. Jack McDuff (piano) lays out in the first 36 measures.

Benson's reading of "Easy Living" consists almost exclusively of block chords with short, single-note connecting lines. The D13♭9 sonority in measure 1 (beat 3) is noteworthy. This chord, a member of the diminished chord family, is moved down *symmetrically* in minor 3rds. The effect is comparable to Johnny Smith's use of a similar device (though his was an ascending phrase) in the classic "Moonlight In Vermont." Benson was, as were most jazz guitarists post-1954, undoubtedly familiar with this chordal maneuver.

Benson reharmonizes "Easy Living" with such enriched changes as: Am7♭5–D7♭9 for F♯° in measures 5, 13, and 29; Bm7–E7♭9 for G♯° in measures 6, 14, and 30; F9♯11 for Am7 measures in 7, 15, and 31. A notable gesture is found in measures 22 and 24. Here he harmonizes the E-F melody with Dm9–E♭m9 chords for a strong coloristic effect. Generally, Benson's choice of voicings and articulation in the tune are reminiscent of his early influences: Barney Kessel, Kenny Burrell, Johnny Smith, and Wes Montgomery. And this is as it should be, as all great jazz is part of an evolving musical tradition which builds on and reaches beyond the work of previous innovators.

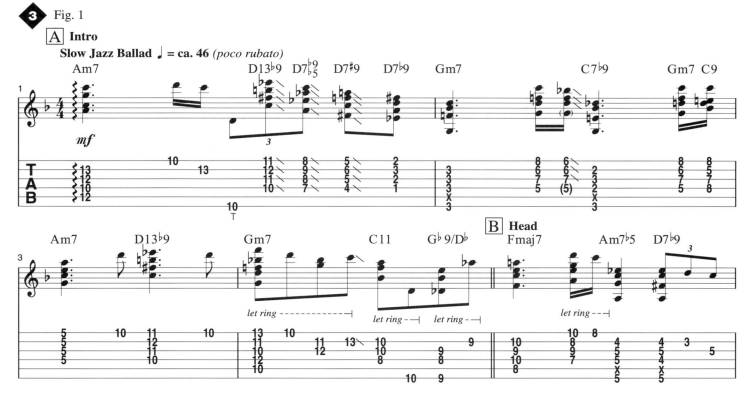

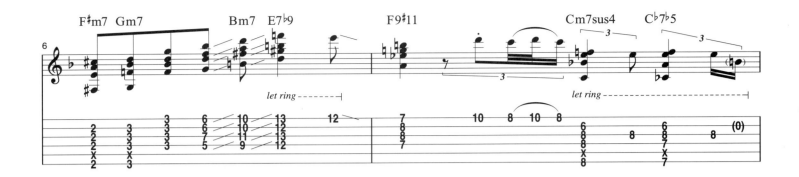

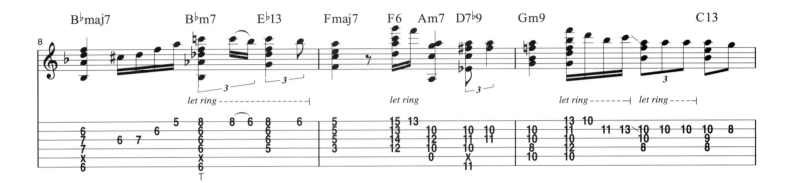

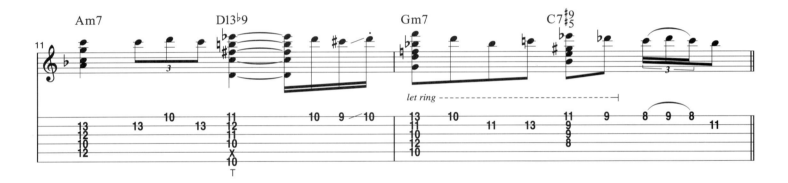

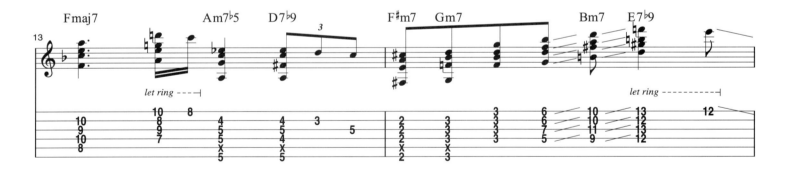

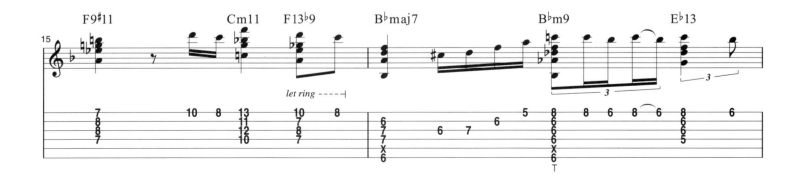

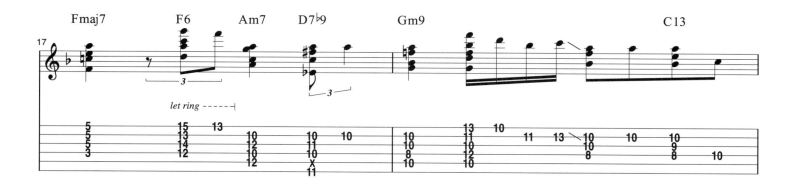

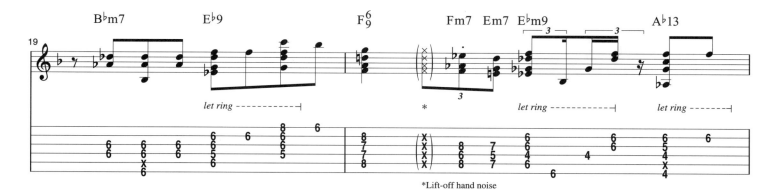

*Lift-off hand noise

1:44 Bridge

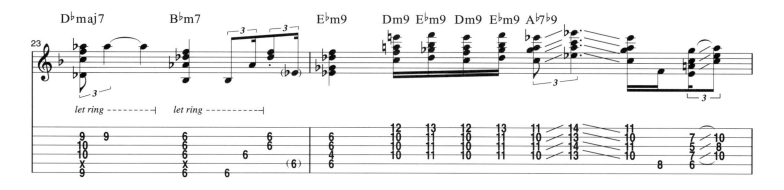

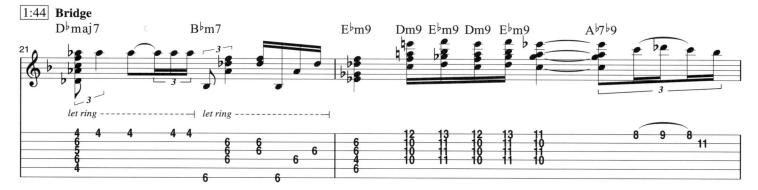

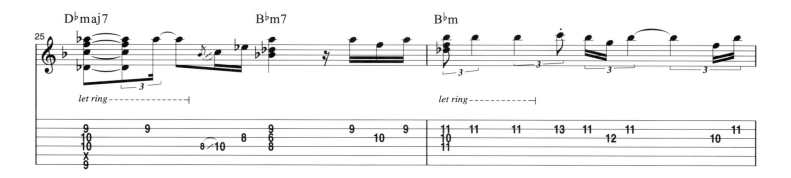

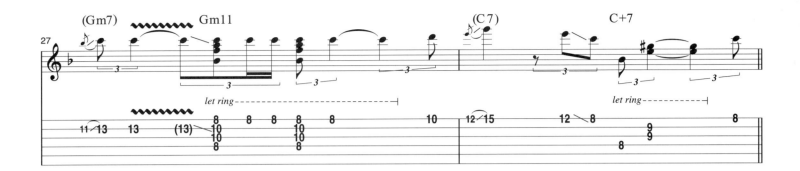

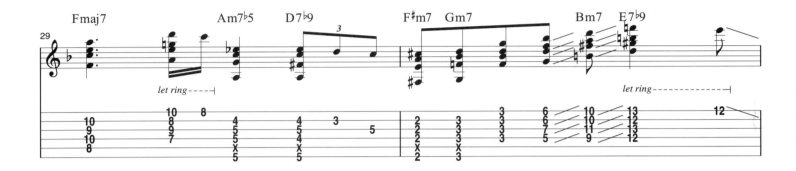

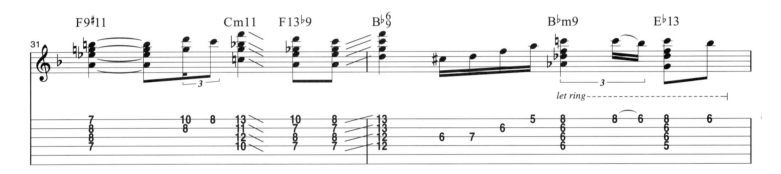

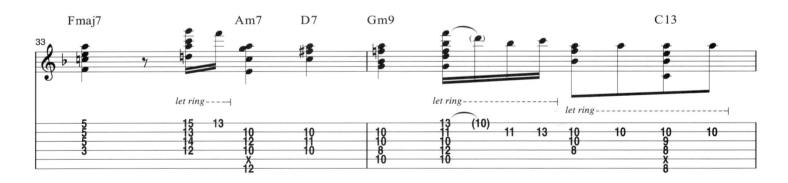

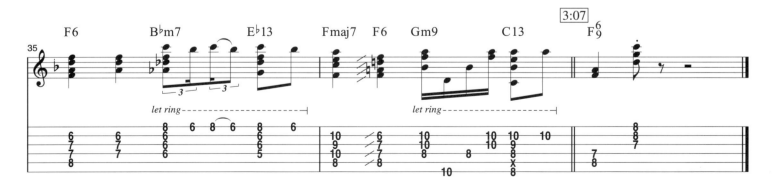

CLOCKWISE
(It's Uptown with the George Benson Quartet, 1966)

By George Benson

Fig.2—Intro and Head

"Clockwise" is the sizzling number that kicked off Benson's *Uptown* set of 1966, his first session with Columbia records. This recording featured Benson's famed combo with Lonnie Smith (organ), Ronnie Cuber (baritone sax), and Jimmy Lovelace (drums). "Clockwise" is an uptempo bop blues typical of his early straight-ahead period when he was determined to make an impression on the jazz world. Indeed he did—largely on the basis of performances like "Clockwise."

"Clockwise" is in G and begins with a terse, rhythmically-charged ensemble figure (Riff A) based on the G Blues scale (G–B♭–C–C♯–D–F) punctuated by G7♯5♯9 and D7♯5♯9 chord bursts. This figure becomes a structural riff in the arrangement, serving as a clever transitional interlude between solos. The head is an attractive blues/bop melody delivered by guitar, organ, and bari sax. An ear-catching episode in measures16–20 outlines four diminished arpeggios filled in with chromatic notes—an affectionate nod to Charlie Christian's "Air Mail Special" solo.

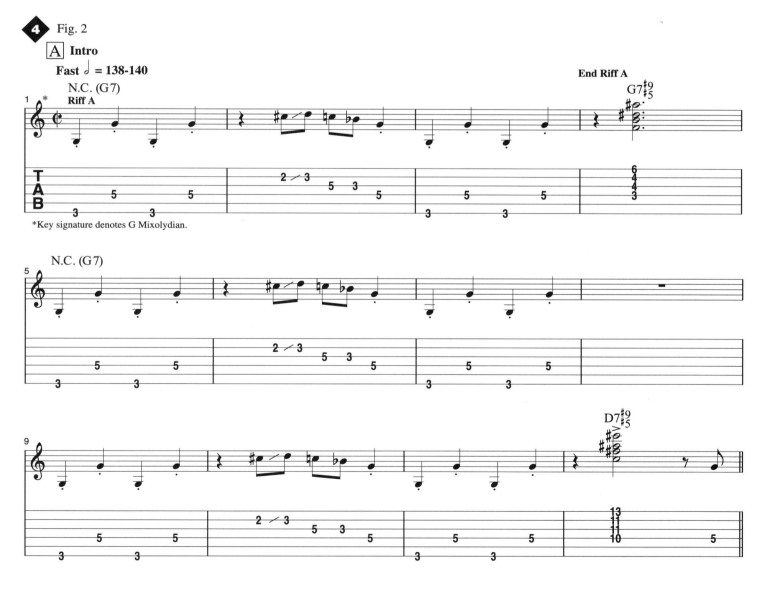

*Key signature denotes G Mixolydian.

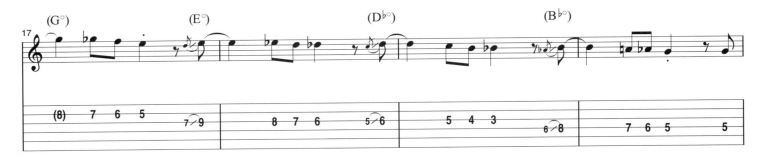

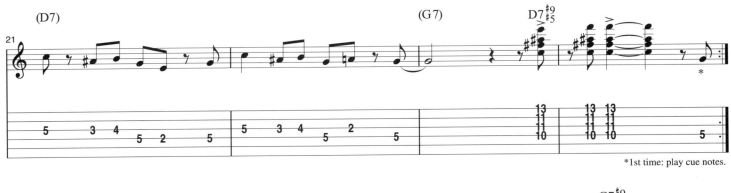

*1st time: play cue notes.

Fig.3—Solo

Benson takes a blistering solo in "Clockwise." The eight-chorus excursion is a dizzying ride marked by his trademark mix of ferocious bebop lines and swinging blues licks. From the opening phrase, Benson adopts a take-no-prisoners attitude with a barrage of complex lines showcasing his immense technical chops. His command of *linear playing* is evident in the maze of position shifts during his improvising, and this linearity remains an important aspect of his guitar technique. Benson uses characteristic slurs (which suit the horn-like conception of his single-note lines) frequently and purposefully throughout the solo. This *legato phrasing* is another identifier of his style.

Benson's improvisations begin in measure 5 on C7, the IV chord. An essential signature lick emerges early in the solo in measure 17. This is a particular descending minor-ninth arpeggio which is ubiquitous in his lines. "The Cooker" (Fig. 5), another fast blues recorded a few months later, also contains several occurrences of this motive. Benson plays variations of the motive in "Clockwise" in measures 21–22, 34–35, 44–45, and 81–82. Additionally, he regularly employs a C minor variant of the motive over C7 to *minorize* the dominant-seventh IV chord. This effect can be heard in measures 17–18, 29–30, and 77–78.

Benson's musical thinking contains numerous advanced harmonic *substitutions*: F minor over E7 in measure 20, E♭ minor over Am7–D7 in measures 21–22, E♭ minor over D7–G7 in measures 34–35, E♭ minor over E7–Am7 in measures 44–45, C♯ diminished as an applied dominant over Am7 in measures 57 and 69, and E♭ major over D7 in measure 82. By contrast, he plays earthy blues licks in measures 12–14, 24–28, 45–47, 48–51, 58–59, 63–67, 70–71, 88–91, and 93–95. These phrases feature Benson's tasteful combining of the G minor pentatonic scale (G–B♭–C–D–F) and the G Mixolydian mode (G–A–B–C–D–E–F). In a similar vein, he plays blues-based groove riffs in measures 23–25, 52–54, 60–62, 72–75, and 84–88. The sequential zigzagging line in measures 80–81, marked by chromaticism and wide-interval jumps, is another highlight. Solos like "Clockwise" cemented Benson's reputation as a precocious master of bop improvisation in the auspicious first phase of his career.

 Fig. 3

E 3rd Chorus

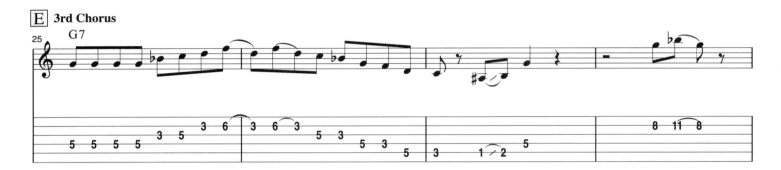

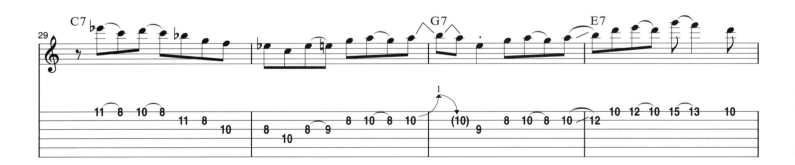

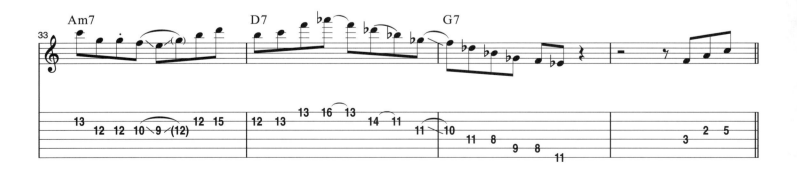

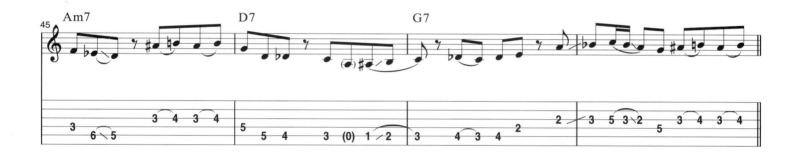

11

H **6th Chorus**

I **7th Chorus**

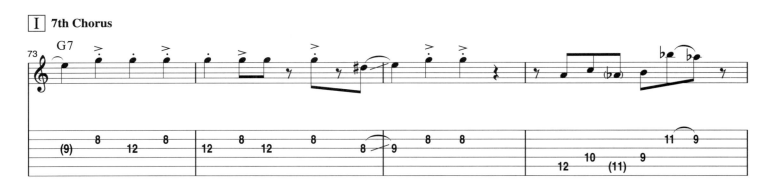

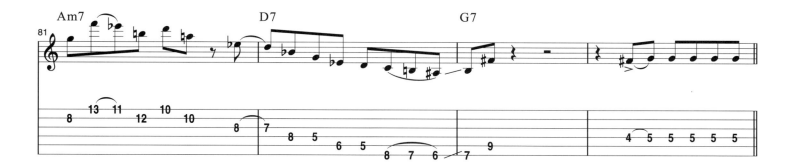

J **8th Chorus**

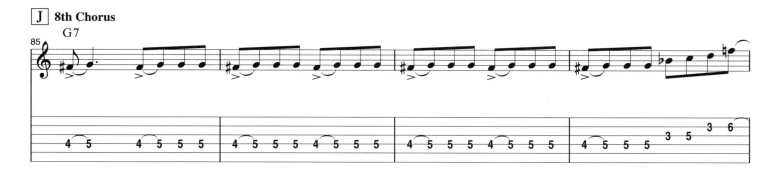

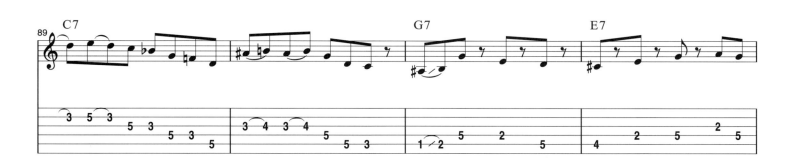

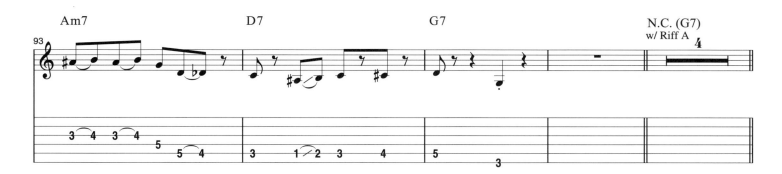

STORMY WEATHER (KEEPS RAININ' ALL THE TIME)

(It's Uptown With The George Benson Quartet)

Lyric by Ted Koehler
Music by Harold Arlen

Fig.4—Solo

George Benson's strong sense of swing pervades his brief solo on the Harold Arlen standard "Stormy Weather." He takes the first thirty-two bars (first two A's of the AABA form) to produce a tight single-note statement that contrasts with the R&B inflections of his vocal. Most of his lines are grouped in strings of eighth notes—typical of bebop phraseology at faster tempi. Benson plays his solo over a repeated Bb–Gm7–Cm7–F7 progression. During its course, he suggests other chords by outlining more harmonically active changes, such as G+7 in measures 14–15. Benson plays characteristic bop substitutions in measures 12 (A diminished over F7) and 16 (Eb minor over F7). Blues licks dominate measures 8–9, 21–23, and 27–28. Throughout the solo, Benson cultivates a lively bopping rhythmic feel, particularly in the bouncy staccato phrasing of chromatic lines in measures 3, 5, 7–8, 17–18, 23, and 30–31. Two versions of a favorite Benson rhythmic/melodic motive crop up in measures 11 and 29. This particular jazz cliché consists of three repeated pitches (quarter–eighth–eighth) followed by a scalar descent or descending minor-3rd jump.

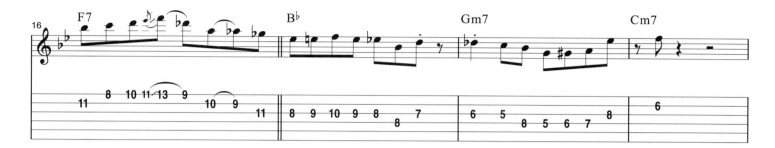

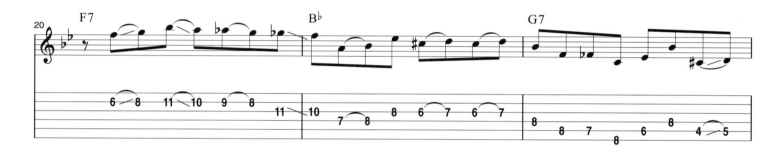

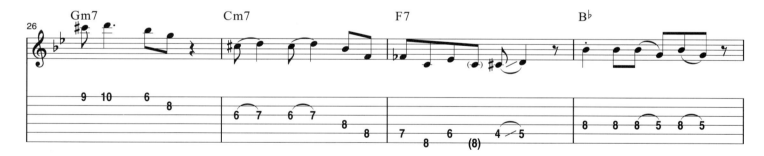

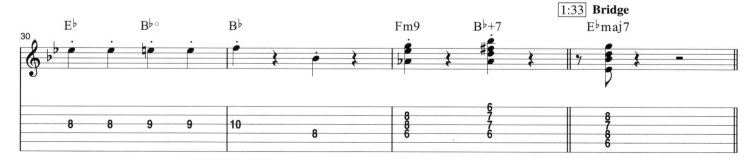

THE COOKER
(The George Benson Cookbook, 1966)

By George Benson

Fig.5—Head and Solo

Benson's crack quartet recorded *The George Benson Cookbook* a few months after *Uptown.* Cut from the same cloth as his previous hard-bop offering, this follow-up effort was distinguished by smoking tracks like "The Cooker." An early signature tune in the Benson catalog, "The Cooker" is an appropriately-titled fast blues in A flat. The 24-bar head (two times through a 12-bar blues), Benson's first seven choruses, and the interlude riff are presented in this excerpt. The head combines single notes and chord punches. Note the use of traditional blues-phrase structure. The repeated four-bar minor-pentatonic melody of the first eight measures is answered by a contrasting melody in measures 9–10. The latter implies a chromatic progression: B♭13–A13, in place of the normally expected ii–V (B♭m7–E♭7) chord change, a clever Wes-inspired permutation.

Benson takes the first solo and comes out swinging at 0:22. Teeming with numerous signature licks, this flight is one of the most exciting of his early period. His opening statement immediately sets the pace with a dramatic rising line which emphasizes harmonically rich tones such as the raised 11th (D), the 13th (F), the raised 5th (E), and the 9th (B♭). Benson plays muscular bop phrases in long strings of eighth notes, a prime identifier of his style, in measures 19–24, 26–30, 33–36, 38–42, 43–48, 54–60, 62–66, and 81–84. These florid lines, reminiscent of John Coltrane's "sheets of sound," are beautifully contrasted by earthy blues licks and groove riffs throughout, as found in measures 50–53, 67–68, and 74–80. Definitive Benson licks appear as phrase endings in measures 36, 48, 60, and 72. He paraphrases a fragment of "All This and Heaven Too" (also a favorite Trane quote) in measures 59–60. By contrast, an R&B-inspired double-stop passage punctuates the solo in measures 69–71. An ostinato of unison bends and bent double stops dominates the seventh chorus before giving way to the ensemble riff in measures 98–108.

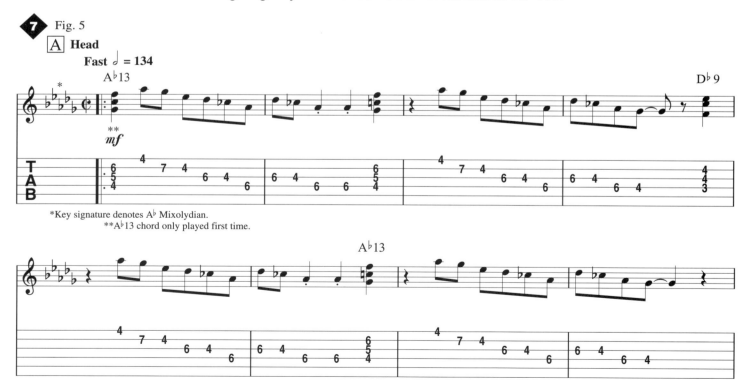

*Key signature denotes A♭ Mixolydian.
**A♭13 chord only played first time.

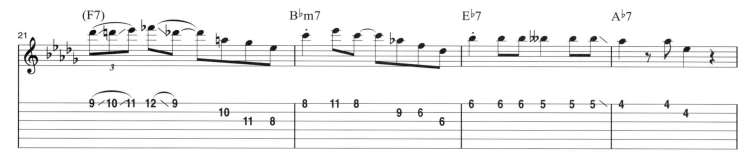

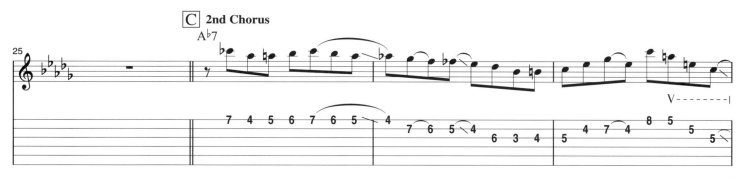

D 3rd Chorus

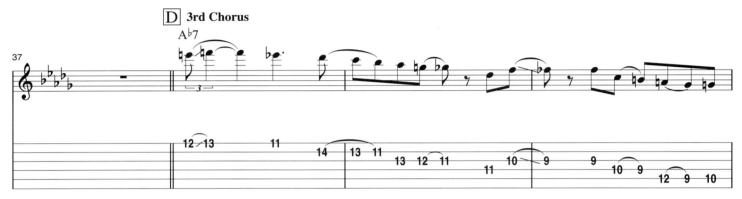

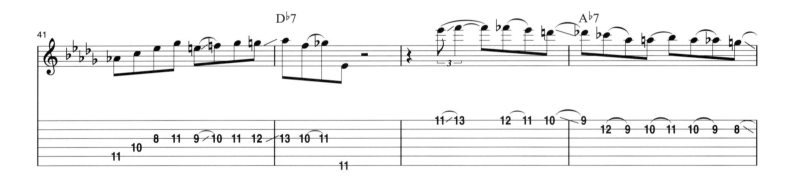

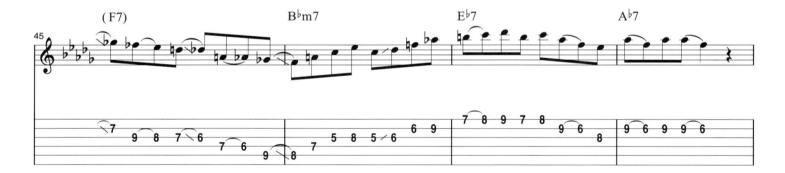

E 4th Chorus

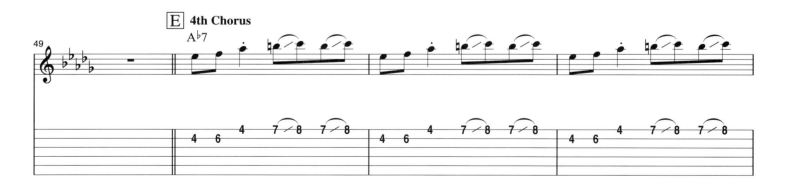

18

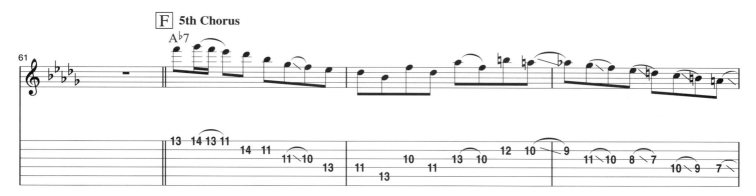

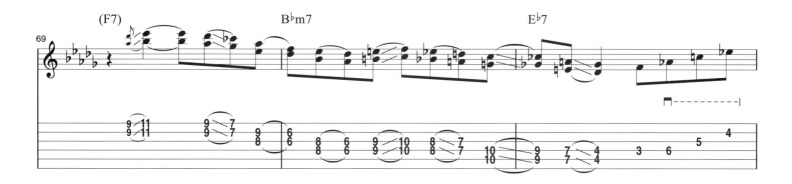

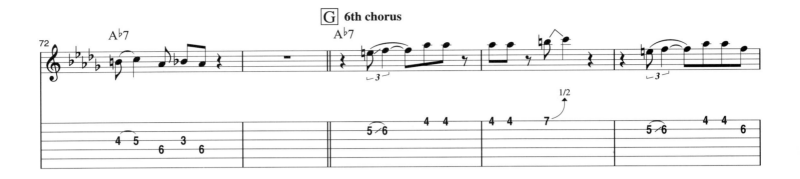

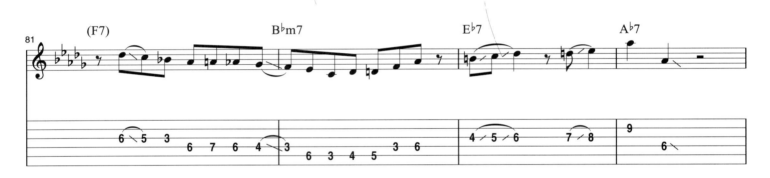

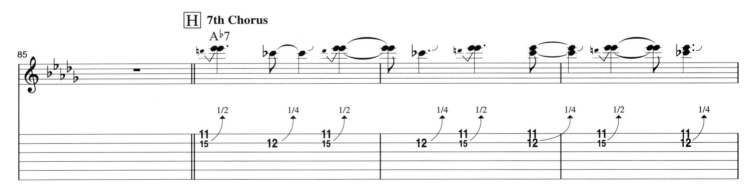

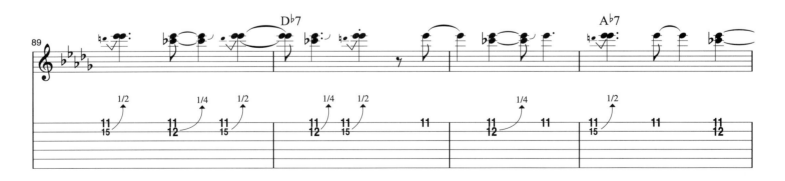

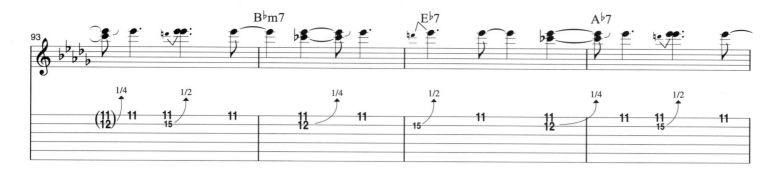

I **Interlude**

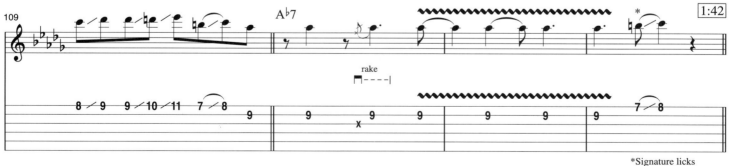

*Signature licks
audio fades out.

THE BORGIA STICK
(The George Benson Cookbook)

By George Benson

Fig.6—Solo

George Benson wrote "The Borgia Stick" for the television show of the same name. His striking solo in the track is a notable highlight of the *Cookbook* sessions. In it, Benson employs an alternation of rhythm feels to maintain musical interest. This procedure would endure to become a regular strategy in his arranging approach for solos, as in "So What" in this volume (see Fig.8). In "The Borgia Stick," Benson sets up the solo choruses as alternating ten-bar sections with six measures of fast swing and four measures of a half-time feel (based on the vamp of the theme).

Benson's solo is in A minor and splits the difference between funky blues, straight-ahead hard bop, and droning modality for a definitive result. Throughout this excerpt, Benson's lines are predominately blues-based and draw from the A minor pentatonic scale (A–C–D–E–G) and A Blues Scale (A–C–D–E♭–E–G). He favors the A Dorian mode (A–B–C–D–E–F♯–G) for modal passages, as in measures 5 and 8. Benson offsets his blues licks with a complex arpeggio-based bop episode in measures 18–20 and the use of the leading tone (G♯) in measures 4, 26, and 36. He plays funky rhythmic riffs in measures 14–15 and 37–39, a familiar ascending pentatonic sequence (also a staple of the rock guitar vernacular) in 28–30, and characteristic broken-dyad lines in 31–34. Benson uses double stops and chordal textures in measures 10–11 and 22 to provide contrast to his single-note lines.

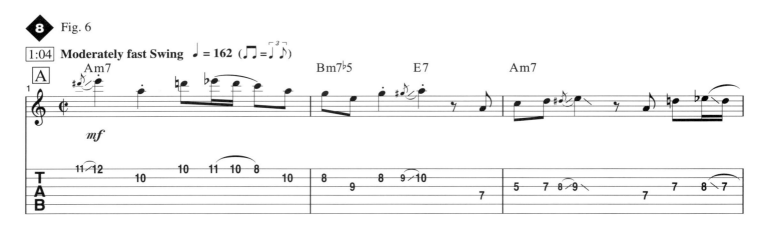

Half-time feel

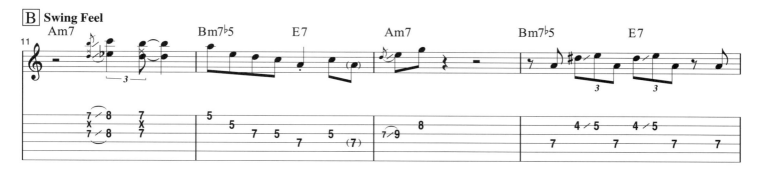

B **Swing Feel**

Half-time feel

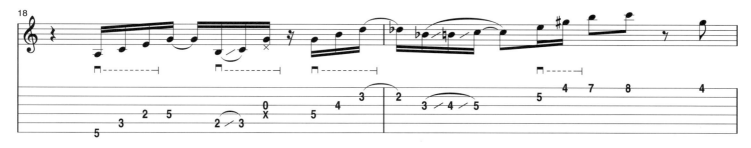

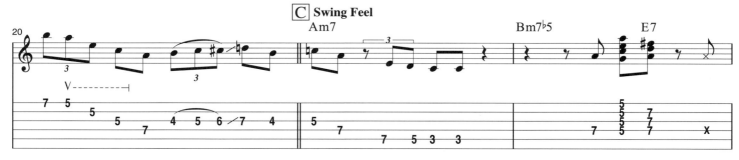

C **Swing Feel**

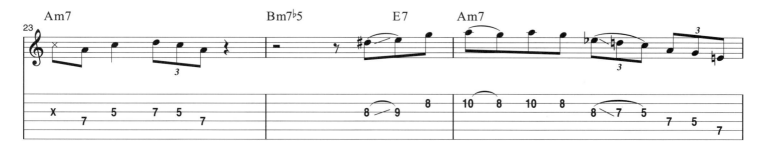

BILLIE'S BOUNCE (BILL'S BOUNCE)

(Giblet Gravy, 1968)

By Charlie Parker

Fig.7—Head and Solo

While George Benson has often been cited as a disciple of Wes Montgomery, he is also as much one of "Bird's children" as most bebop saxophonists. He transferred much of Charlie Parker's vocabulary and phrasing to the guitar. Harnessing his formidable technique, he was able to execute these daunting sax lines with an unprecedented fluidity and fire. Benson paid homage to Bird with a superb rendition of the classic blues, "Billie's Bounce," during his stint with Verve Records in the late 1960s. The sessions featured the era's luminaries of jazz: Herbie Hancock (piano), Ron Carter (bass), Billy Cobham (drums), and Johnny Pacheco (percussion). This undoubtedly drove Benson to greater heights.

Benson and company play "Billie's Bounce" in the original key of F. His unusual arrangement builds gradually. The twelve-bar melody acts as both intro and theme statement. It is played twice in the head [A] [B], first in unison with the bass (backed only by percussion), and then with a contrapuntal guitar-bass treatment. Benson plays the first two solo choruses [C] [D] with a similar sparse backing. Drums and piano enter in the third chorus [E].

Benson's improvisations start in [C]. His rhythmic phrasing, command of the instrument, and mastery of the musical language yield a mature and potent bop solo. You'll hear Bird-inspired bebop lines in measures 44–46, 50, 67–71, and 104–108, augmented by more dissonant, chromatically-tinged substitutions and angular phrases in measures 26–27, 56–57, 63–64, 80–82, 92–93, and 115–117. Benson paraphrases the "Honeysuckle Rose" lick, a valuable bop improviser's cliché, in measure 93. Groove riffs typical of swing music provide contrast in measures 36–43, 47–49, and 96–103. Benson plays double-note blues figures associated with pianists and organists in measures 34–35 and 97–101. The latter phrase combines keyboardish mannerisms with blues-guitar double-stop bends for a beautifully balanced effect.

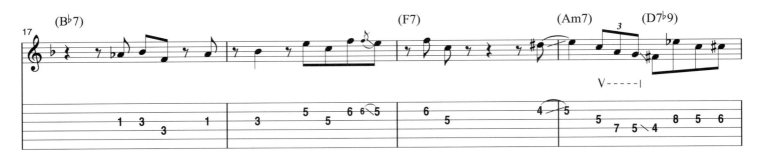

0:26

C Solo: 1st Chorus

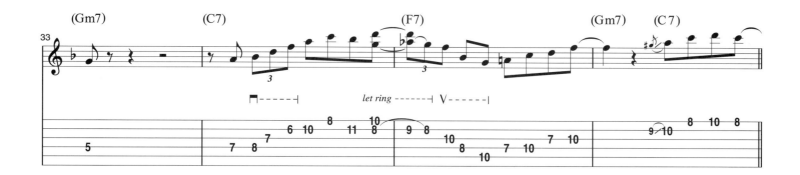

D **2nd Chorus**

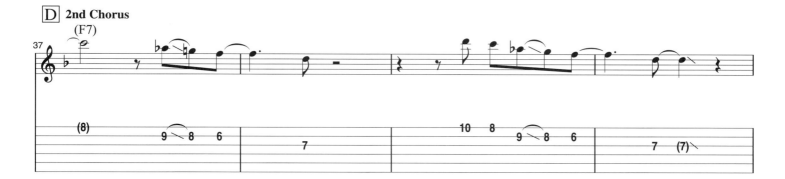

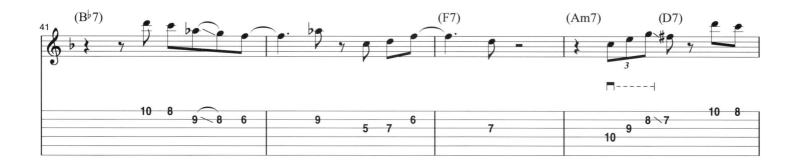

E **3rd Chorus**

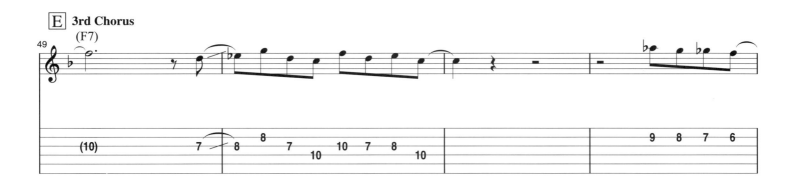

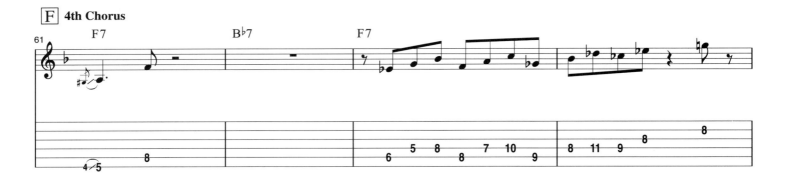

F 4th Chorus

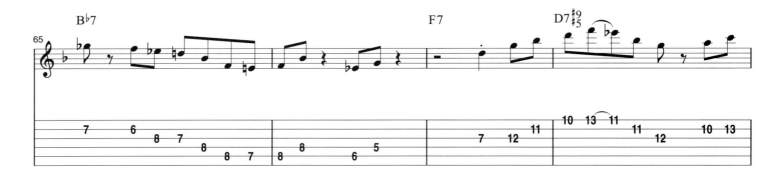

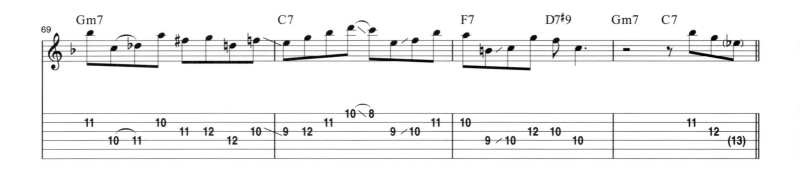

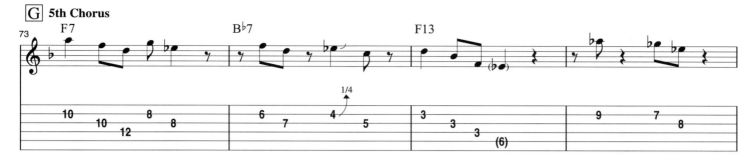

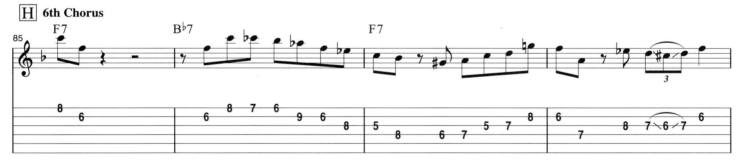

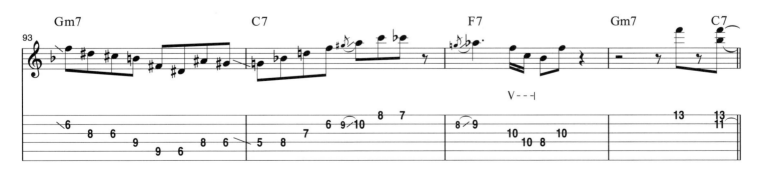

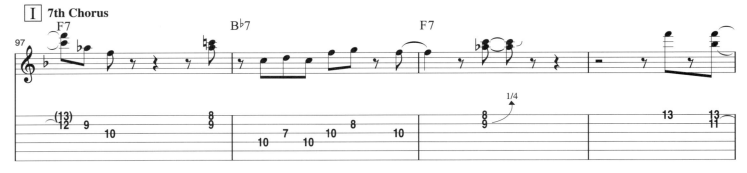

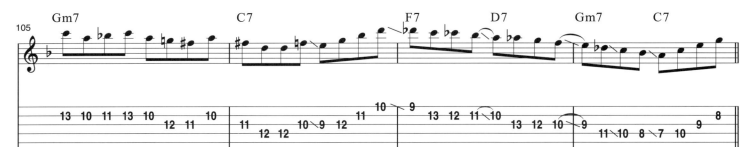

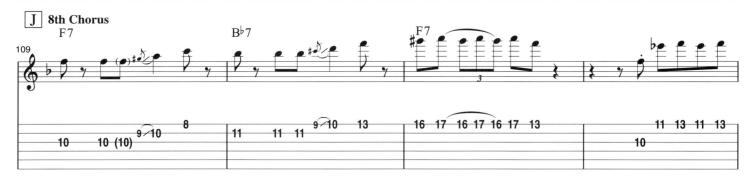

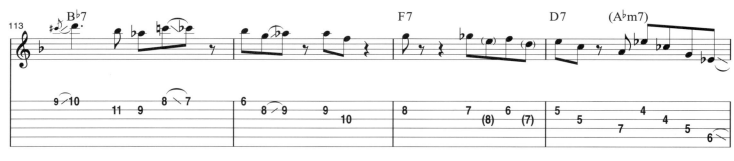

SO WHAT

(Beyond The Blue Horizon, 1971)

By Miles Davis

Fig.8—Solo

George Benson began recording for the new CTI (Creed Taylor, Inc.) label in 1970. He appeared as a sideman on records by trumpeter Freddie Hubbard and tenor saxophonist Stanley Turrentine before making his 1971 debut as a leader with *Beyond the Blue Horizon*. The personnel consisted of Ron Carter (bass), Jack DeJohnette (drums), Clarence Palmer (organ), and Michael Cameron and Albert Nicholson (percussion). Benson's cover of "So What" was a stand-out track from the set. The guitarist had previously recorded with Miles Davis (*Miles in the Sky*, 1968) and now breathed new life into what is arguably the most well-known Davis tune.

Benson's "So What" solo is a career milestone providing a new take on the modal jazz classic. The tune itself, however, presented a problem—how to say something new within the limitations of its modal parameters. The "So What" chord changes behind the solo are static and move in slow harmonic rhythm through D minor and E flat minor modal centers. To generate greater musical interest and allow for a broader exposition of styles, Benson arrived at a novel solution: He devised a unique arrangement to contain the improvisations. The solo choruses alternate feels and tempi in this scheme: a rock feel with a heavy backbeat ([A] and [D]), fast swing in cut time ([B] and [E]), and medium swing ([C] and [F])—a constantly changing six-chorus form. Benson tempers his ideas and adjusts his phrasing to reflect the mood of each chorus. Throughout his improvisations, he mixes funky jazz-rock and blues-based licks with mutated bebop phrases and dissonant "outside" lines.

The first chorus [A] connotes a rock attitude, based on pentatonic and blues-scale licks and straightforward Dorian-mode melodies. The second [B] exposes the bop face of Benson's style with more elaborate high-velocity lines. The third chorus [C] exploits bluesy triplet rhythms, groove riffs, and a climactic slurred phrase. The fourth [D] returns to a rock feel with shorter fragmented licks and funky double stops. The fifth chorus [E] elaborates on his earlier bop lines and contains a dramatic across-the-barline trill in measures 112–113. The final chorus [F] is riff-dominated, distinguished by blues licks and an ostinato based on slurred three-note chords (a Benson signature) in measures 118–125. Benson plays bop phrases in long strings of eighth notes in measures 20–27, 35–40, 80–86, and 87–95. He superimposes extended chord sounds and substitutions in measures 21–22 (A7$\flat$9$\sharp$5), 23 (Bm7$\flat$5), 26–27 (Cmaj7), 84–85 (A7$\flat$9$\sharp$5), 87 (B$\flat$m7), and 92 (Fm maj9), all over D minor. Benson departs from the basic modality of the moment in the post-bop "outside" playing of measures 6–7, 11–13, 52, 69–71, and 86–88.

10 Fig. 8

A **Solo: First Chorus**

Rock feel

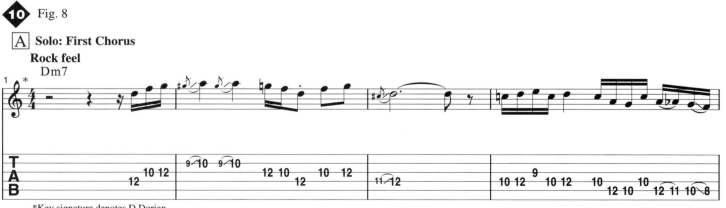

*Key signature denotes D Dorian.

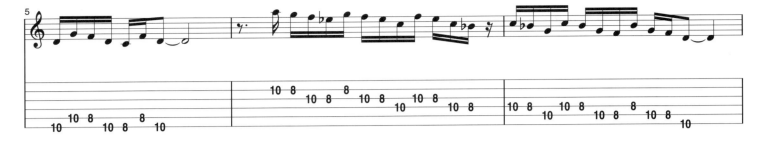

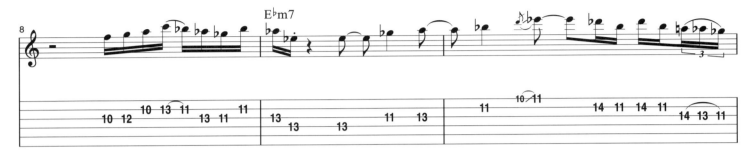

B Second Chorus (Fast swing) ($\downarrow = \downarrow$)

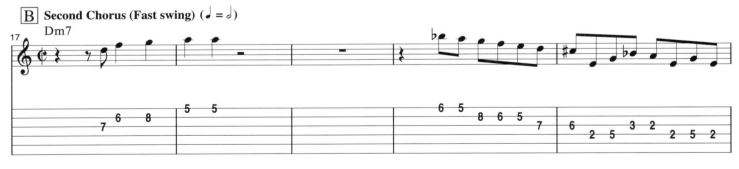

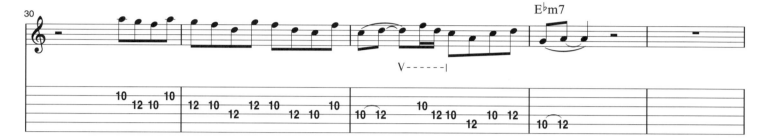

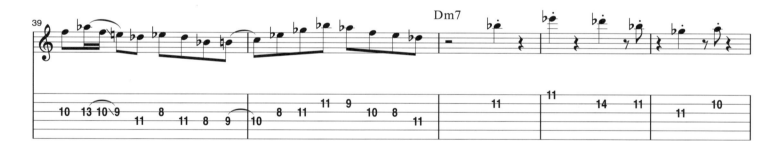

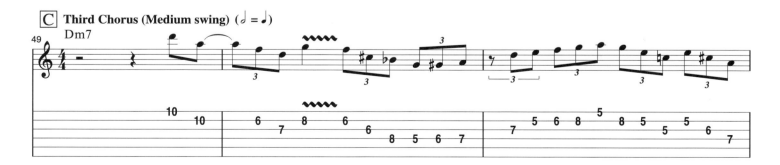

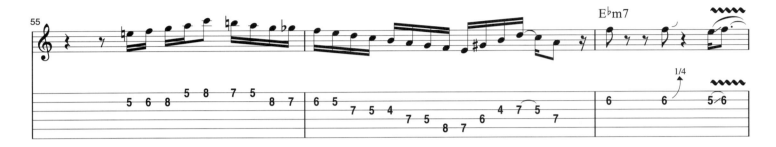

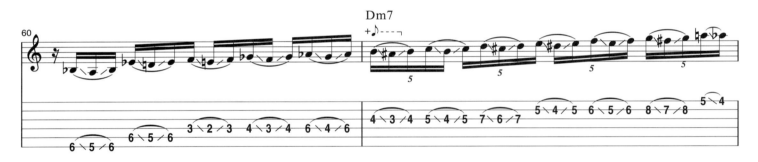

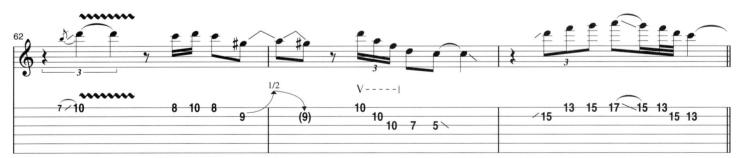

D **Fourth Chorus (Rock feel)**

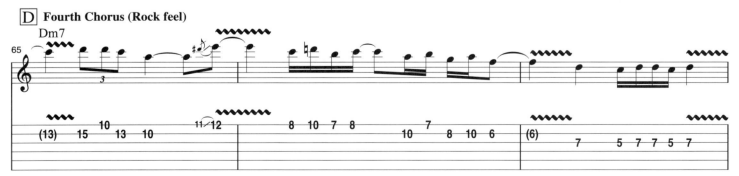

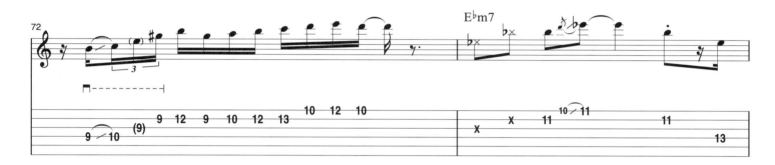

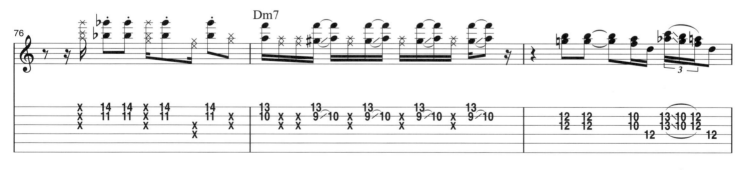

E Fifth Chorus (Fast swing) (♩ = ♪)

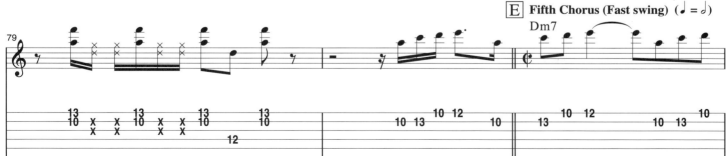

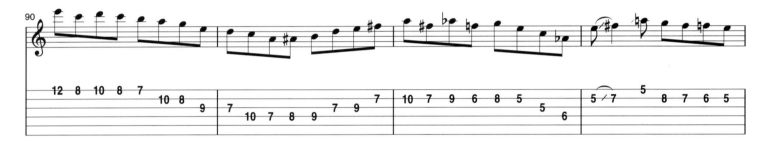

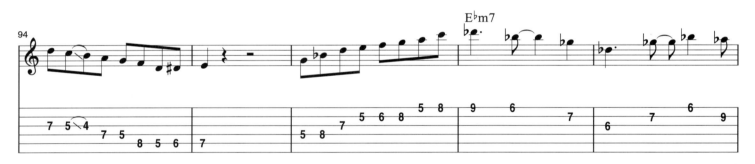

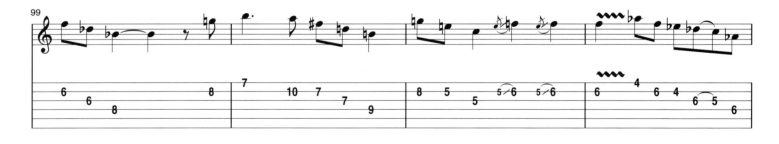

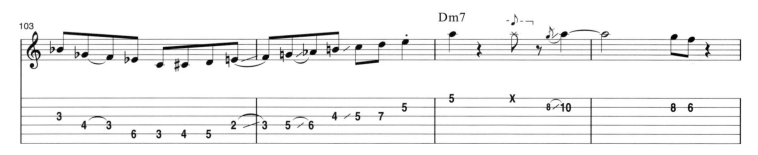

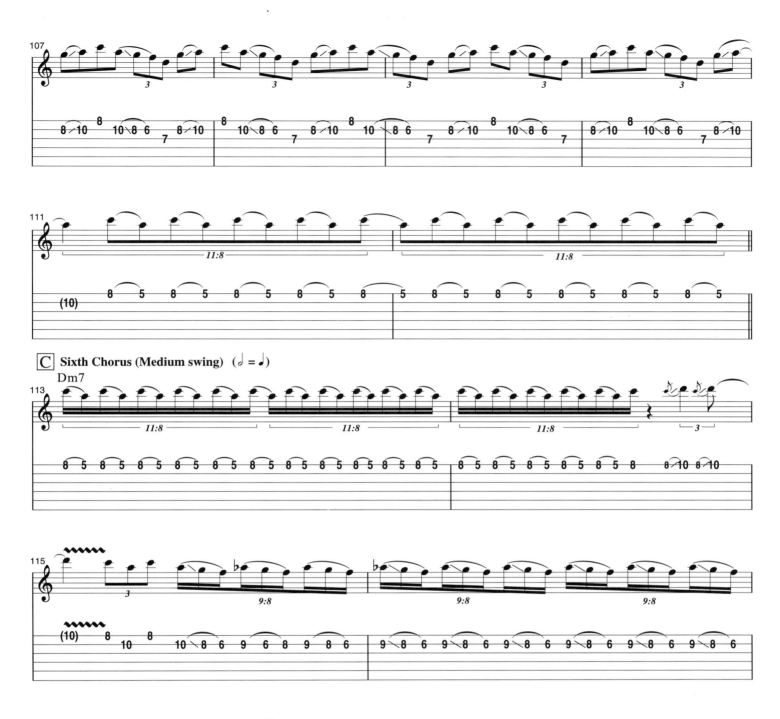

C Sixth Chorus (Medium swing) (♩ = ♪)

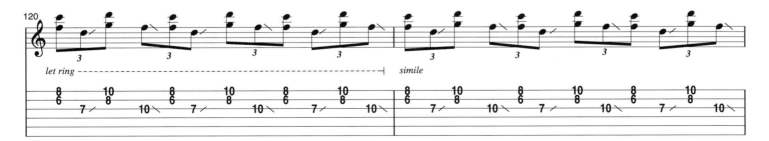

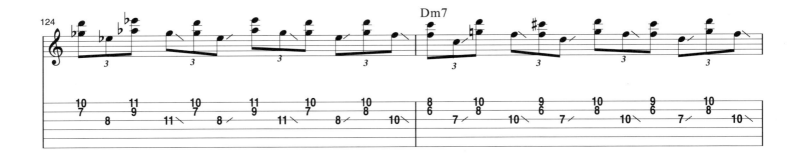

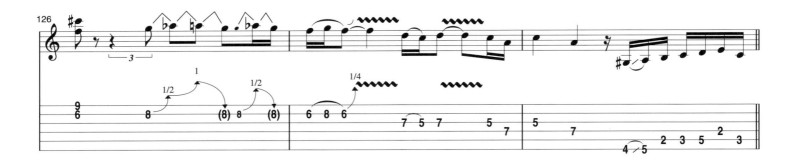

H Interlude (Rock feel)

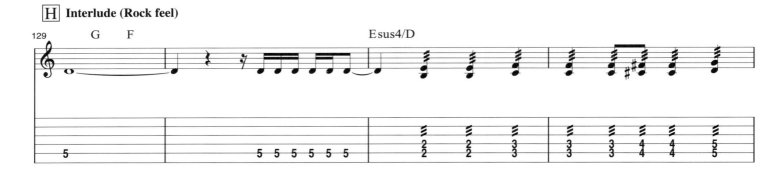

*Tremolo pick w/ steady gliss.

BODY TALK

(Body Talk, 1973)

By George Benson

Fig.9—Intro and Head

The mid-1970s CTI period saw Benson further expanding his musical horizons beyond bop and modal jazz in the *Body Talk* recording. The sessions boasted an impressive lineup: Ron Carter (bass), Jack DeJohnette drums), and Harold Mabern (electric piano), augmented by a first-rate horn section and the presence of then-upcoming guitarist Earl Klugh. The title track is an exemplary grooving Benson composition that captures his fusion of jazz, funk, Latin, blues, and rock idioms. A riff-based tune planted solidly in E (the Mixolydian mode: E–F♯–G♯–A–B–C♯–D), "Body Talk" relies on a simpler harmonic language and a static tonal center, more typical of rock vamps than chord changes. A thematic ostinato figure (Riff A) played by piano and bass dominates the intro. Benson joins the arrangement in measure 5 with a strong secondary riff, reminiscent of the "Tequila" theme. He plays the figure in the first position, utilizing its unique timbre and making strategic use of open strings.

Benson introduces the first theme in measures 9–12. This is a bluesy gospel-inspired chord riff made of triads and dominant seventh chords. Note the trademark voicing of the E7/D chord: an octave (D–D) with an inner sixth (B). Benson has employed this sonority often, using its ambiguous nature to good advantage for a variety of harmonic situations. The tune's second (and more prominent) theme in measures 17–28 exploits these distinctive voicings to an even greater extent for E7/D, A/C♯, D/A, E/G♯, D/F♯, and A/E chords. The second theme comes to a close in measures 27–28 with a blues-swing figure based on a *minor-sixth pentatonic scale* (E–F♯–G–B–C♯).

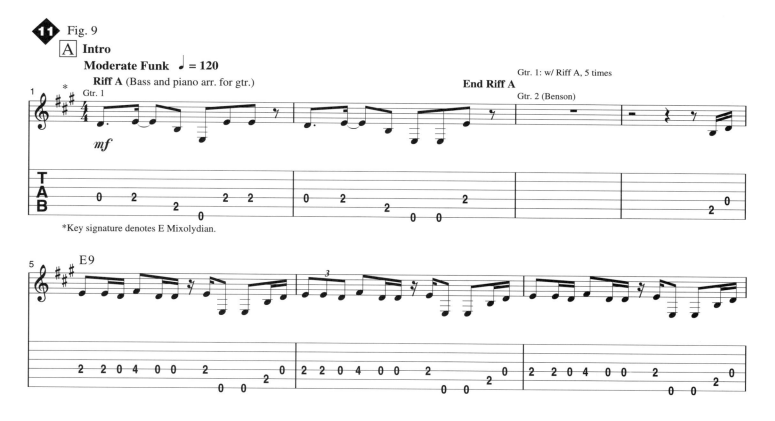

Fill 1

Fill 2

Fig.10—Solo

Benson plays his solo over an ostinato in E—essentially the song's main riff. He crafts a definitive statement from a mix of funky blues licks, mutated bop lines, and utterly unique chordal passages. During this phase of his CTI period, Benson regularly explored varied textures as a strategy in improvising. Note the variety of ear-catching chordal phrases in measures 7–8, 12–15, 17–20, 40–44, 56–63, 71–78, and 83–84. The highly original Benson figure in measures 75–78 is particularly noteworthy. This is a driving rhythmic riff made of parallel minor 3rds (on the second and third strings) with an upper D note on the first string, implying Em7 and A11 sounds.

Benson utilizes a blend of blues, funk, and jazz elements in his single-note lines. An unusual *oblique-motion* voiceleading motive appears in measures 11 and 55. This consists of a rising chromatic line and a *pedaled* upper E note. Benson employs repeated notes and pedal tones in the energetic riffs of measures 21–25, 37–39, and 63–69, and blues and funk licks in measures 5–7, 26–28, 44–48, and 70–71. His modal-jazz side surfaces in the use of B minor (Dorian mode: B–C#–D–E–F#–G#–A) sounds over the E Mixolydian tonal center, as found in measures 10 and 33–36. By contrast, Benson plays more complex bop-oriented lines in measures 10, 29–32, 49–53, and 81–82. He flirts with atonality in measure 52 and makes use of angular intervallic shapes in 53–54.

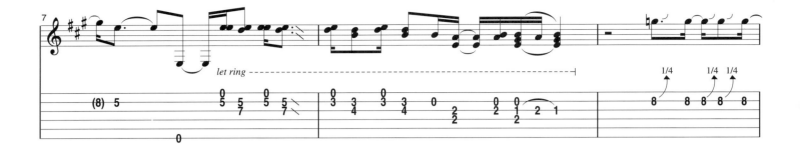

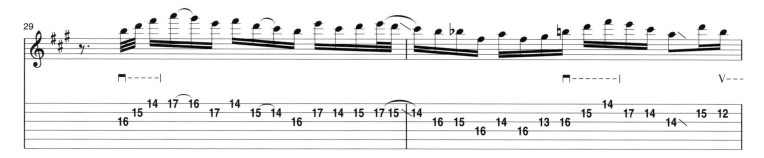

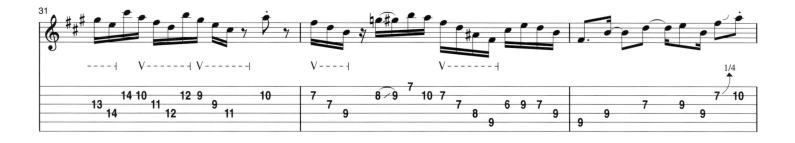

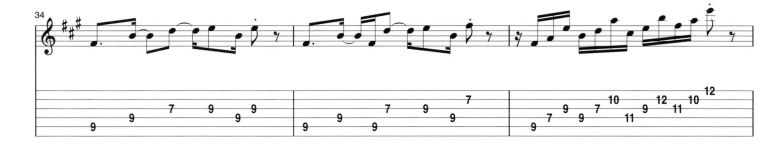

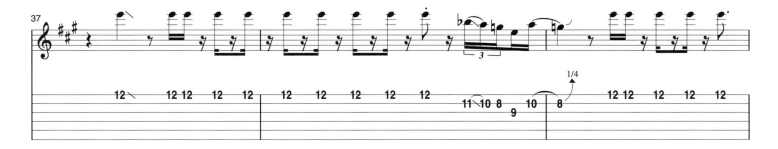

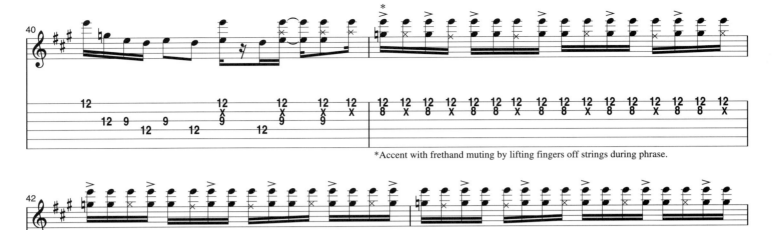

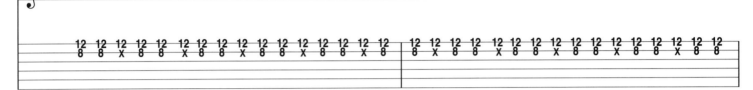

*Accent with frethand muting by lifting fingers off strings during phrase.

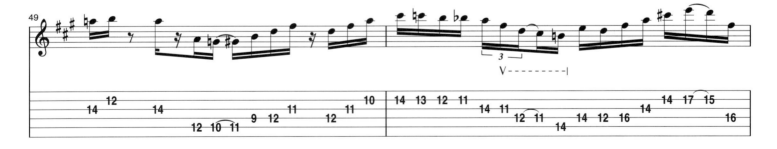

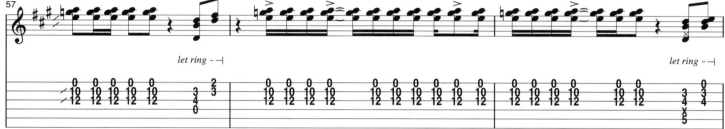

**Strum while sliding.

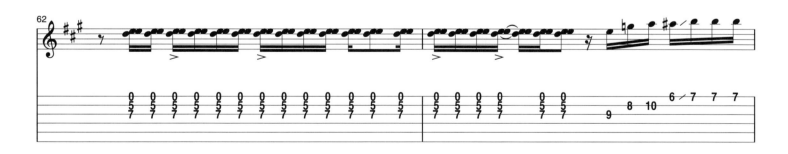

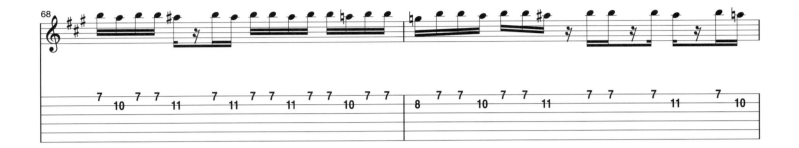

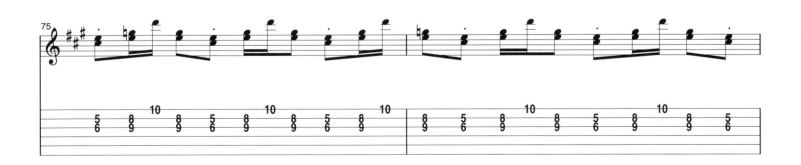

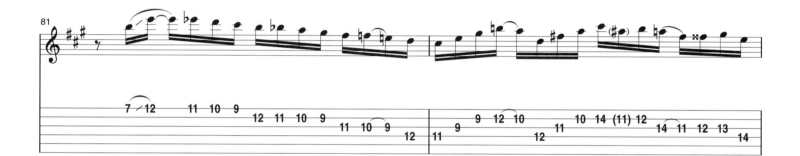

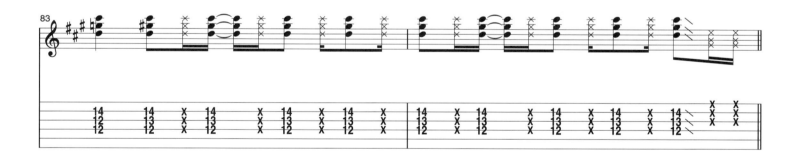

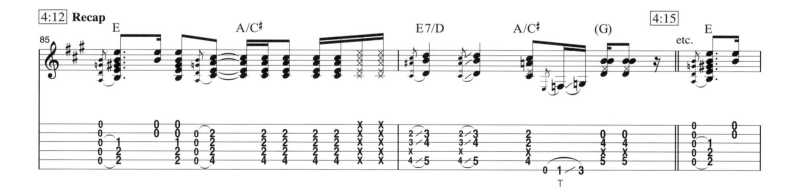

TAKE FIVE
(Bad Benson, 1974)
By Paul Desmond

Fig.11—Intro, Head, and Solo

Many consider Benson's next CTI release to be his finest of the period. *Bad Benson* featured a new band and a revitalized reading of "Take Five." The lineup consisted of Phil Upchurch (rhythm guitar), Kenny Barron (electric piano), Ron Carter (bass), and Steve Gadd (drums). "Take Five" is the "cool jazz" classic (a 1961 Top 40 hit by the Dave Brubeck Quartet) that introduced millions of listeners to odd meter. This rendition grew out of a demo Upchurch arranged and played for Benson. In this arrangement, Upchurch introduces, establishes, and propels the 5/4 groove with a solid R&B rhythm figure (Rhy. Fig.1). Benson enters in the fourth measure and states the head in single notes with typical embellishments. Note the use of slurred ornaments in the main theme (Theme 1), as well as his "fall offs" (horn-inspired downward slides) in the secondary theme (Theme 2).

Benson begins the solo with sparse melodies and space, generating forward motion through increasing activity, thicker textures, and various rhythmic devices. Note the use of rhythmic motives in measures 29–31 and 35–39. Benson's lines are generally modal, based on both the E♭ Dorian mode (E♭–F–G♭–A♭–B♭–C–D♭) and the E♭ minor pentatonic scale (E♭–G♭–A♭–B♭–D♭). Benson plays a signature episode of *broken-octave* dyads in measures 33–40. He plucks these two-note chordal lines with the fingers (or pick and fingers). The quick minor-pentatonic riffs in measures 41–43 are staples of Benson's funk style. Pentatonic riffs give way to more complex, double-timed sixteenth-note strings in measures 44–51. Benson weaves several bop elements into his lines: chromaticism in 47 and 48, references to the altered dominant chord (B♭7♭9) in measure 48, and seventh and ninth chord arpeggios (G♭maj7, A♭9, B♭m7) in measures 48–50. Benson plays two unmistakable licks in this section. The first, in measures 48–49 (beats 5-3), involves a rising major seventh arpeggio, an interval leap of a 4th preceded by a "leading tone" (E–F–B♭), a descending chromatic passing tone (F♭), and a conclusion with a Bird-inspired bebop figure (beats 2 and 3 of measures 49). The second, in measure 51, often played as a phrase ending, is a descending two-octave A♭ minor ninth arpeggio (E♭–C♭–B♭–A♭). A return to dyad texture provides further contrast in measures 52–56.

13 Fig. 11

A Intro

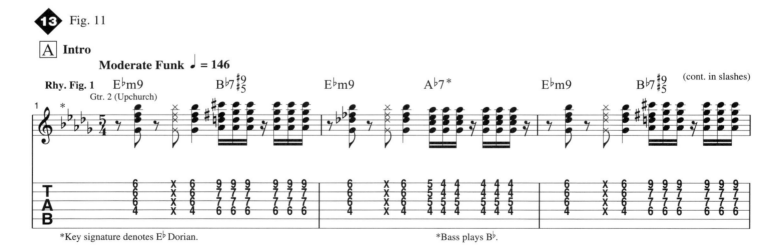

*Key signature denotes E♭ Dorian.   *Bass plays B♭.

Sweet Georgia Brown

PLAY 11 CHORUSES ♩=234

Words and Music by Ben Bernie, Maceo Pinkard and Kenneth Casey

1

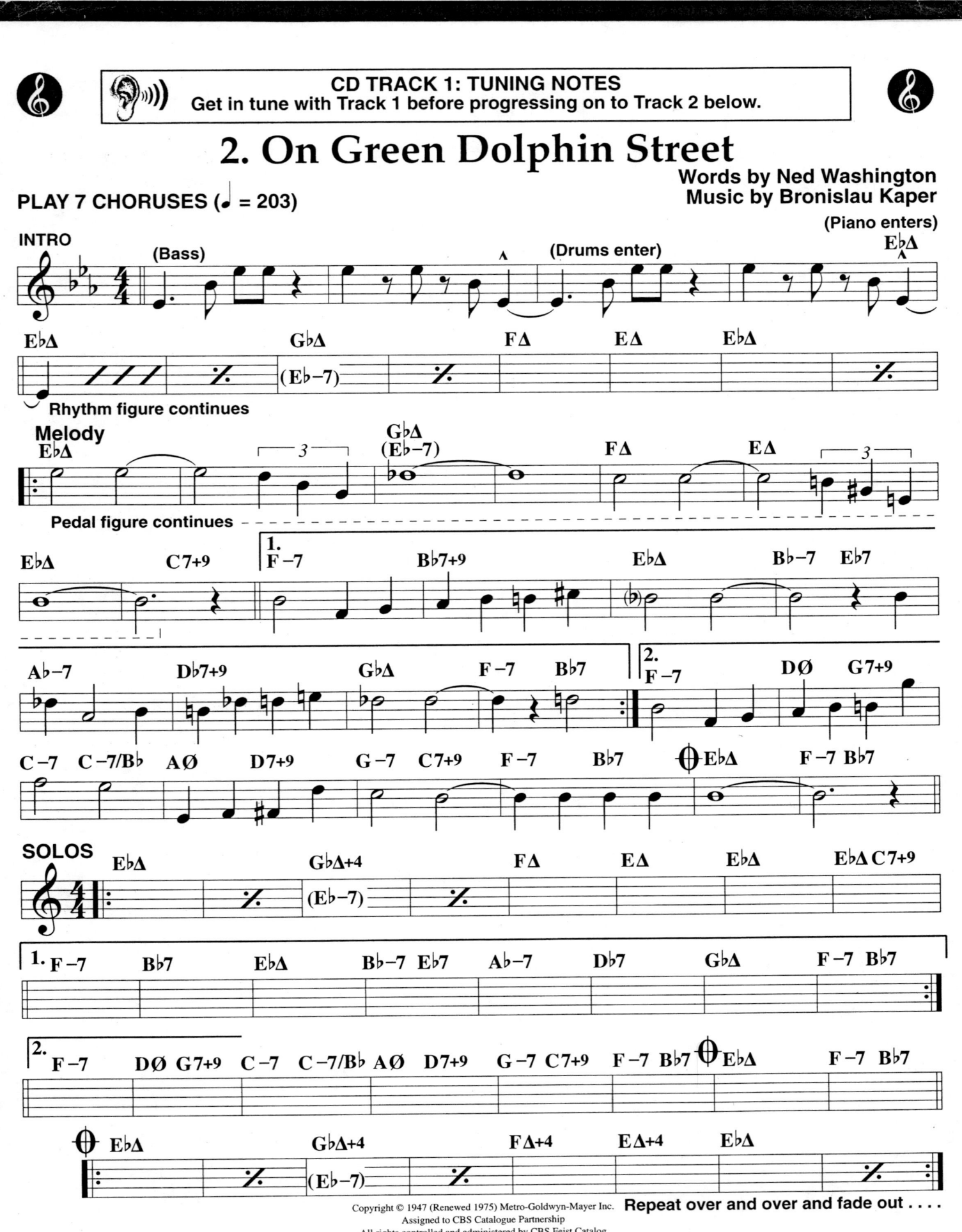

THE VERY THOUGHT OF YOU

RAY NOBLE

Ballad

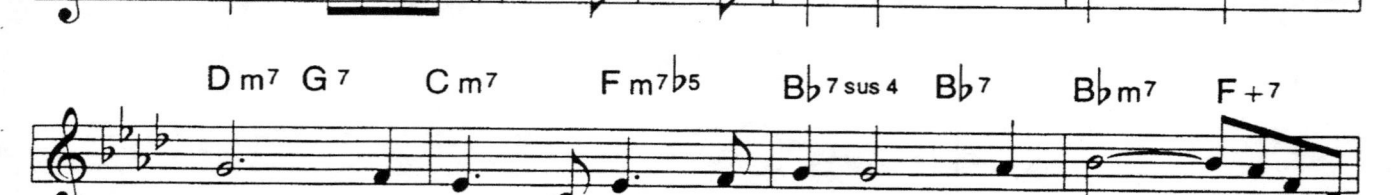

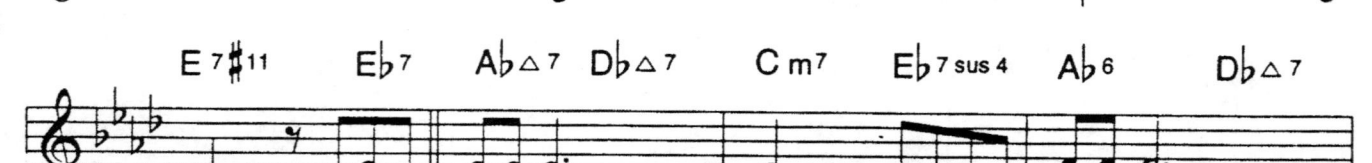

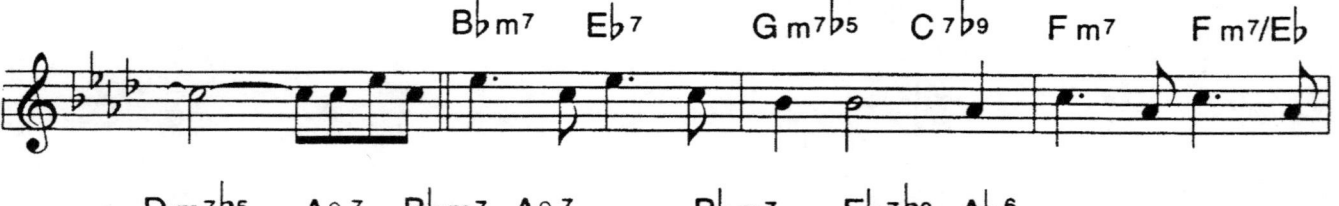

Brian Newland
is BURNT!!

3. Just Friends

GUITAR PRACTICE RECORD

Week of _Aug 23rd_

MON	TUES	WED	THURS	~~FRI~~ MON	~~SAT~~ TUES	~~SUN~~ WED	THURS
	· Ornithology ✓ (Half step parts) & (accidental!)		All Blues ✓	Take Five · Benson solo · Learn Bridge Chords	Take Five · Benson solo · Bridge Chords · Bridge melody Octave up	Bossa Dorada · Melody · Comping	Ornithology · Solar · method title
	Django tune ✓		Ornithology · Head – dilfer · Guide Tones	Ornithology · Head · Guide Tones	Bossa Dorada · melody · Comping	Green Tea	Django waltz
	Vicente Años		Django Tune	Bossa Dorada	Ornithology		Bossa Dorada
	"All Blues" Julian Lage solo		Veinte Años	Green Tea	✻ Pick tunes + play Thursday ✱		Solar
							Julian Lage
							Triste

Joyspring

· Alone Together
  · Ornithology
  - Blue Work
  - Straight, No chaser

B Head (Theme 1)

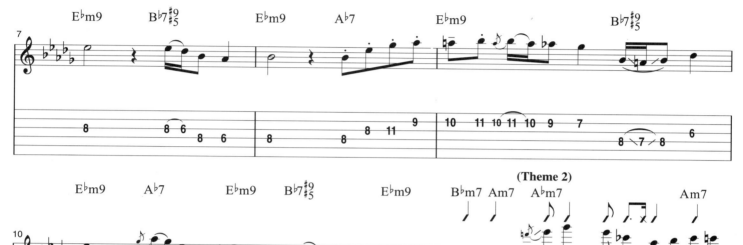

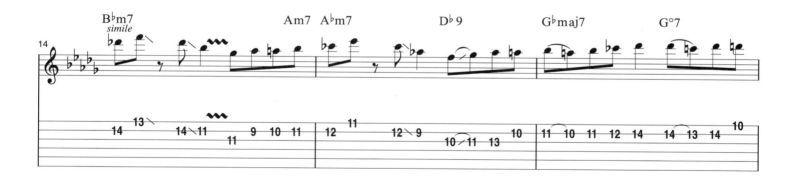

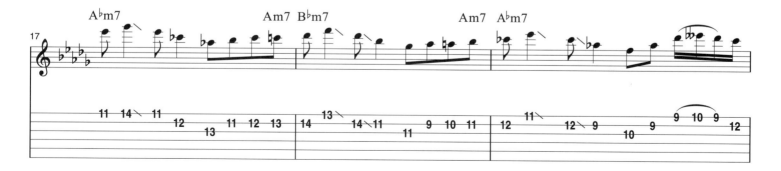

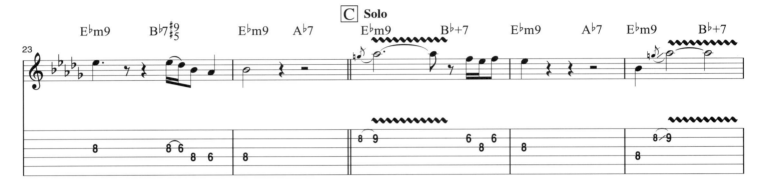

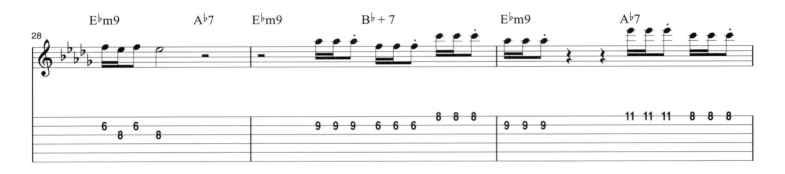

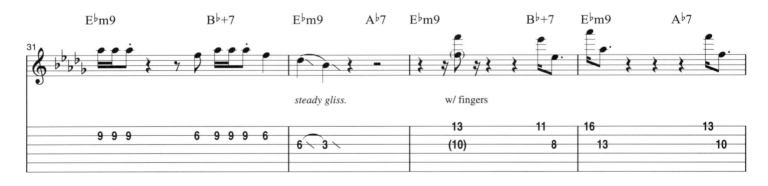

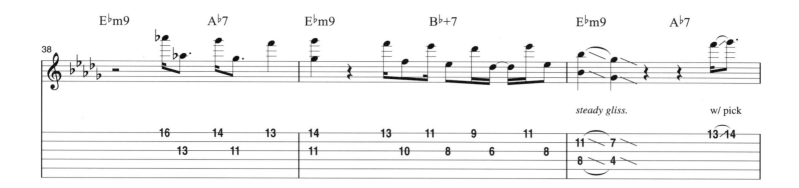

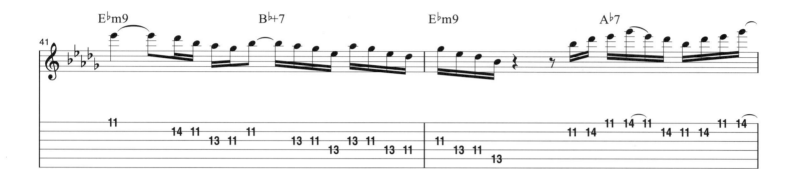

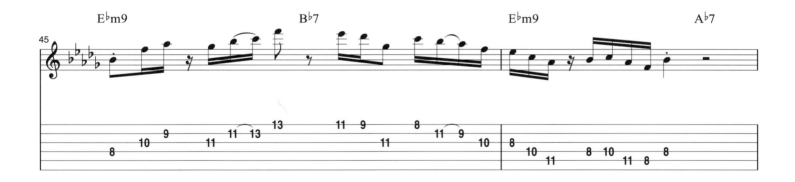

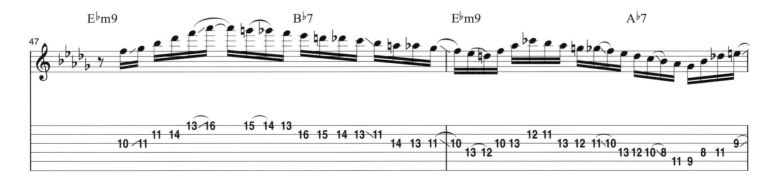

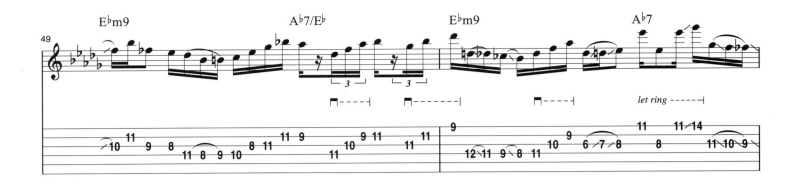

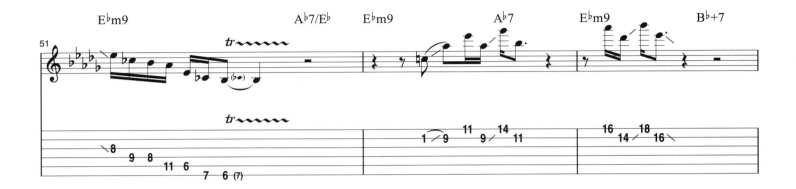

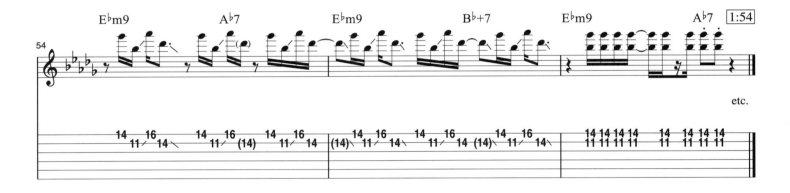

BREEZIN'
(Breezin', 1976)
By Bobby Womack

Fig.12—Intro, Head, and Solo

George Benson's 1976 *Breezin'* album was an artistic and commercial triumph. Blurring distinctions between pop, jazz, R&B, and dance music, this was the release that introduced jazz guitar to the masses and made Benson an international star. *Breezin'* found the guitarist at the height of his powers with a new label (Warner Bros.) and a new band (which again included cohort Phil Upchurch). The title track was a Bobby Womack composition originally written for guitarist Gabor Szabo. It became the perfect vehicle for Benson, who transformed it into the guitar anthem of the late 1970s. The winner of Grammies for Record of the Year and Best Pop Instrumental, "Breezin'" foreshadowed both the funky pop-jazz movement and the smooth jazz genre to follow.

The "Breezin'" intro [A] is built on a funky riff in D which outlines a D–Bm7–Em7–A7 progression. The head is made of three distinct sections. The first theme [B] is stated as simple parallel 3rds joined midway by doubling flutes. These 3rds imply the upper extensions of the chords, Dmaj9 and Em9. The second theme, [C] and [E], is a singable melody firmly situated in D major. The third theme [D] is a funkier, more rhythmic section and makes use of single-note major-pentatonic licks and trademark Benson chord phrases in measures 57–65. Note the *octave-plus-inner 5ths or 4ths* voicings of these three-note chord shapes.

Benson's definitive solo [F] exemplifies his amalgam of traditional jazz and modern funk idioms. He alternates blues-based groove riffs and light rock licks with modal jazz and occasional quick diatonic flurries, as found in measures 109 and 136–139. Benson plays modal lines, also of the diatonic type, in measures 84–85, 104–106, and 111–118. He exploits groove riffs, often containing characteristic repeated-note figures, in measures 87–90, 91–92, 119–120, and 124–128 and uses bluesy string bends in the licks of measures 86–87, 92–95, 98–102, 121–124, and 140. Benson plays a D minor-pentatonic flurry as a phrase ending in measure 129. Many of his funkier lines juggle minor and major sounds in a manner consistent with blues and swing harmony. Note the evocative melodies throughout that place 6th (B) and 9th (E) tones in the D minor-pentatonic context. The solo culminates with a partial recall of Theme 3 in measures 141–148 before a full-fledged return to Theme 2 [G] begins in measure 150.

Benson went out on a limb during the recording sessions. He achieved the unmistakable guitar sound on *Breezin'* with a new and untried combination: a Gibson Johnny Smith guitar and a Polytone amp.

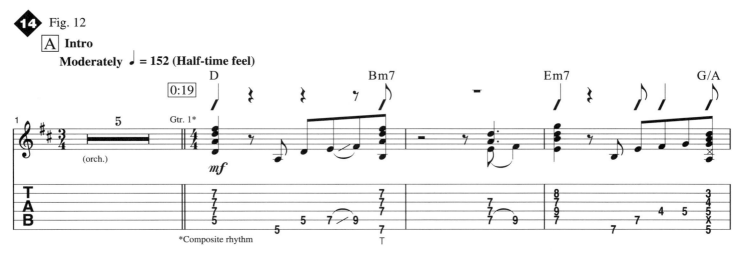

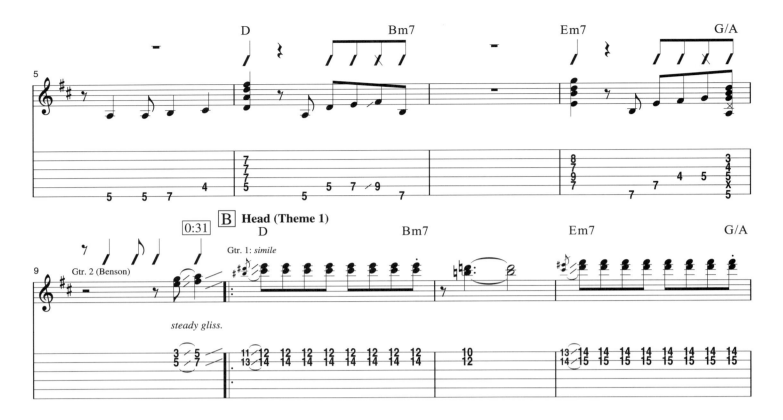

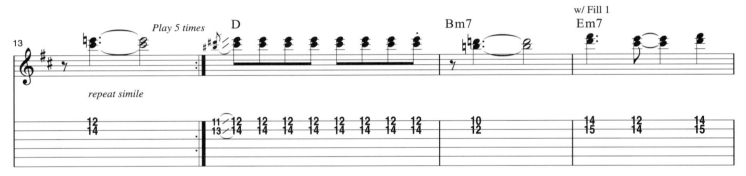

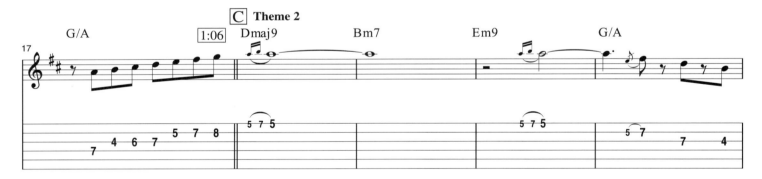

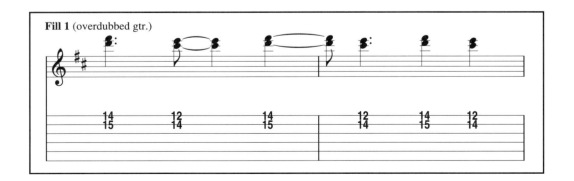

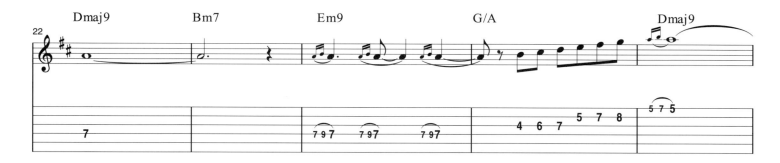

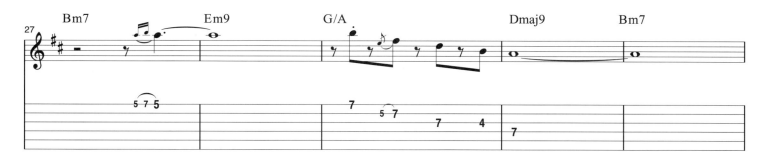

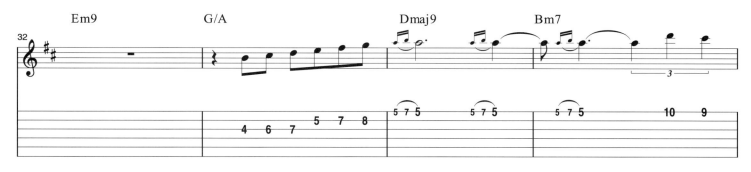

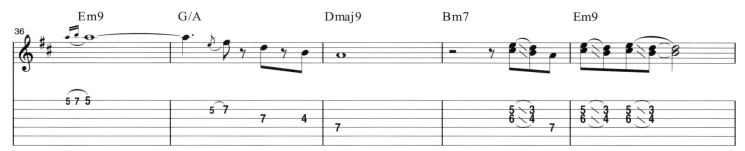

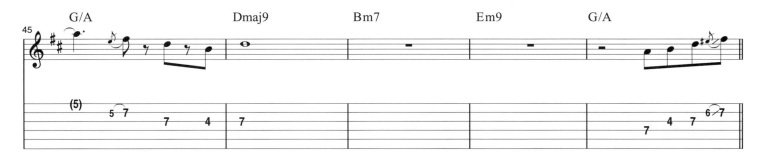

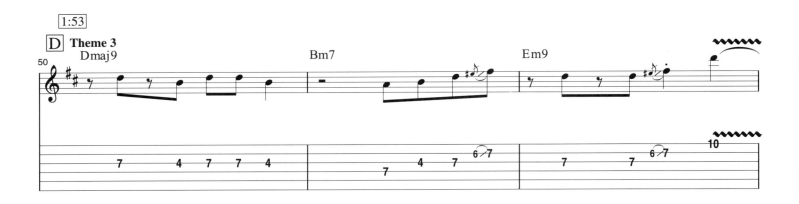

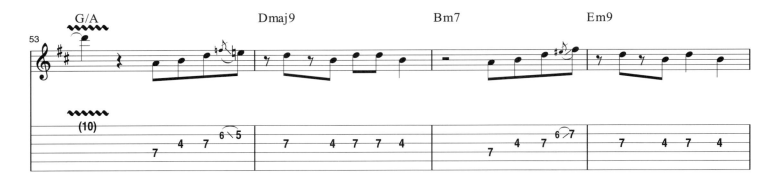

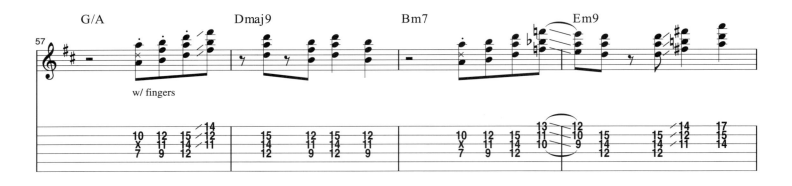

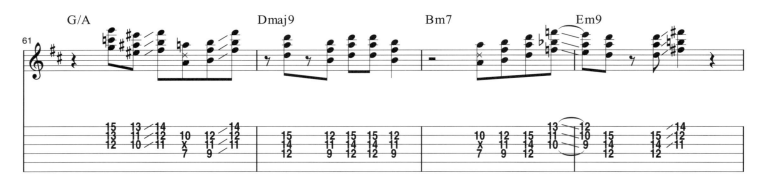

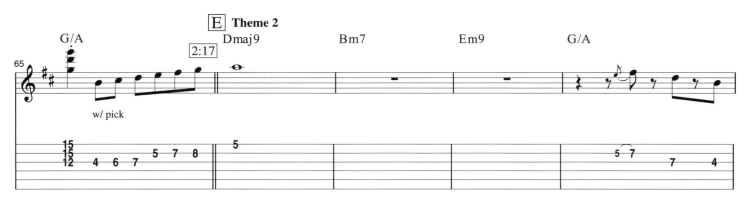

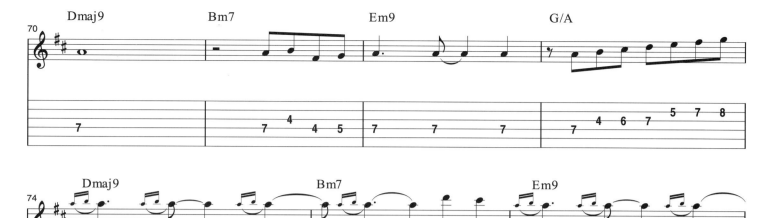

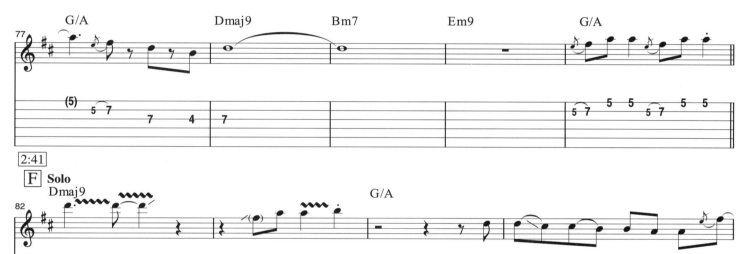

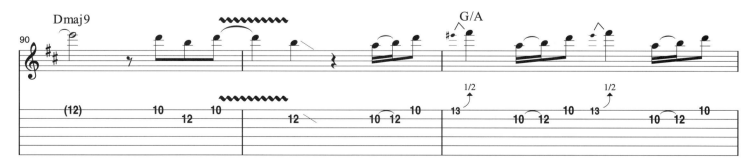

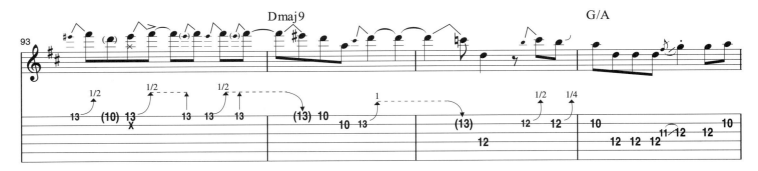

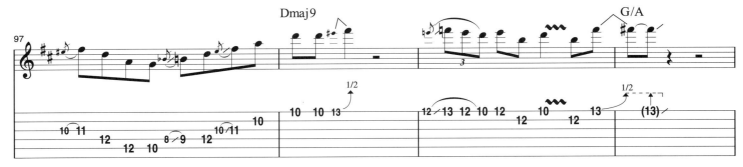

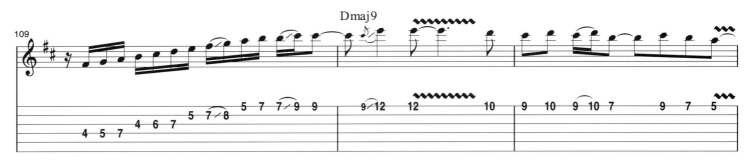

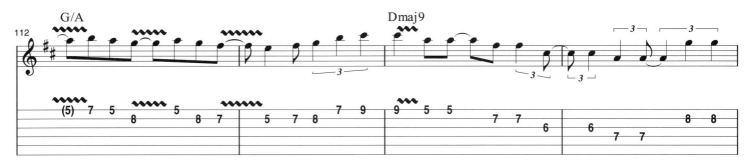

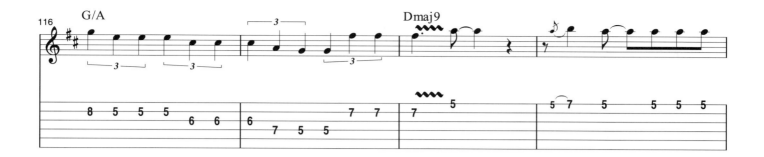

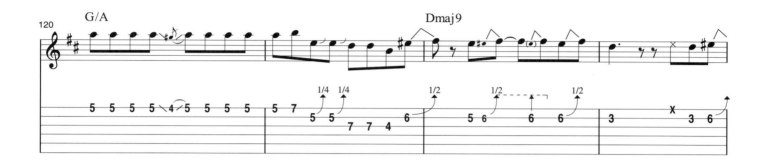

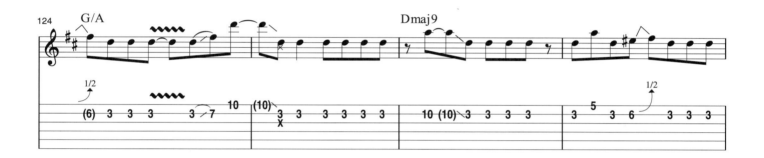

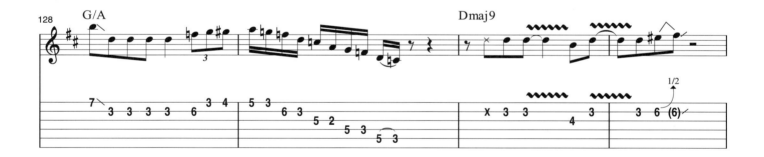

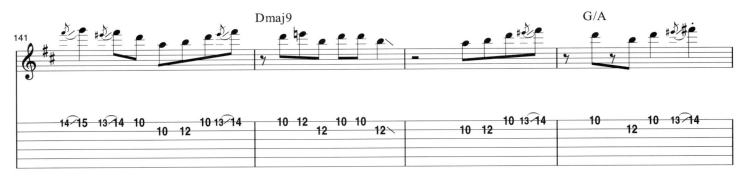

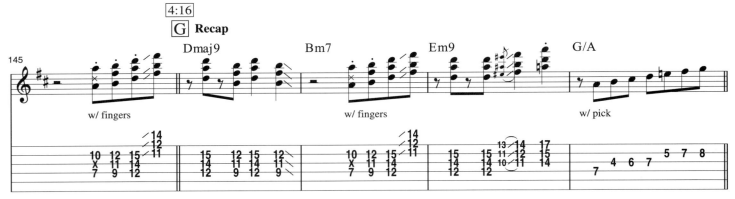

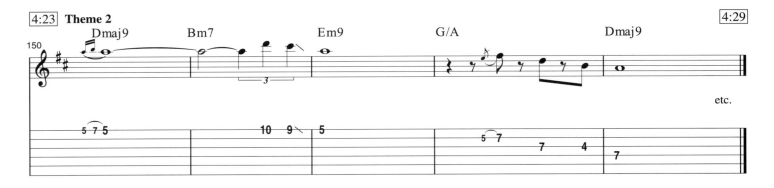

THIS MASQUERADE
(Breezin')

By Leon Russell

Fig.13—Solo

Breezin' was the first jazz album to sell over one million copies. One significant factor in its popular success was the mega-hit "This Masquerade," the 1976 Top 10 single that launched Benson's monumental pop career. Pop concessions and commercial concerns aside, the Leon Russell-penned tune featured some of Benson's finest guitar work. Case in point is his attractive blues-tinged solo at 3:23. Benson doubled much of this improvisation with wordless vocal lines for a unique quasi-duet effect. This scat-vocal/guitar effect became a significant aspect of his style and an identifier of future performances.

Benson plays the solo in a mid-tempo groove over an Fm7–B♭7 vamp. Most of his lines split the difference between minor blues and funk. He draws heavily from both the F Dorian mode (F–G–A♭–B♭–C–D–E♭) and the F blues scale (F–A♭–B♭–C♭–C–E♭). Benson emphasizes the 9th (G) throughout in prominent lines and at climactic points in his improvisation, as in the opening phrase. He plays signature minor-ninth arpeggio licks in measures 10 and 19. Riff-based thinking pervades much of the solo, especially in the repeated figures in measures 10–13, 26–29 and 30–32, and the trademark winding pentatonic sequences in measure 18. Benson employs bluesy string bends in 15 and 20–21. He changes texture and punctuates the largely single-note statement with chord bursts in measures 24–26, and his closing episode of descending parallel 3rds in measures 35–38.

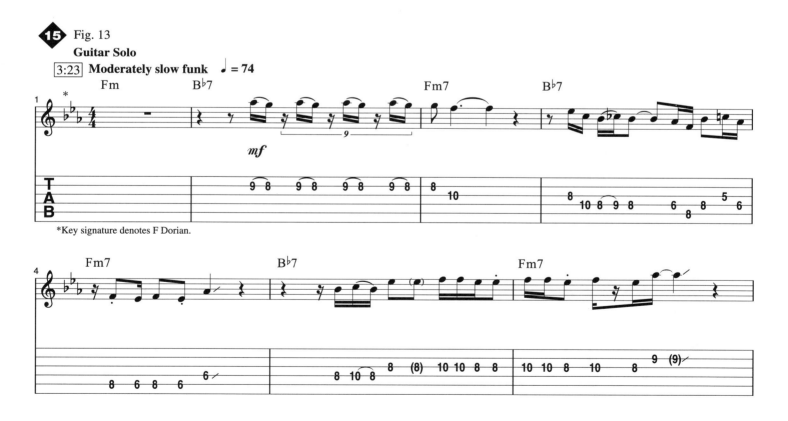

*Key signature denotes F Dorian.

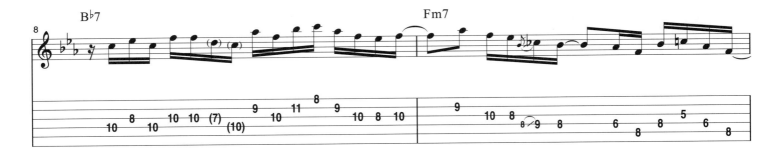

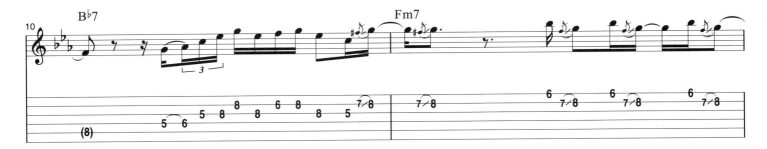

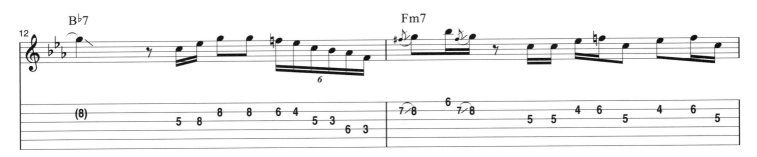

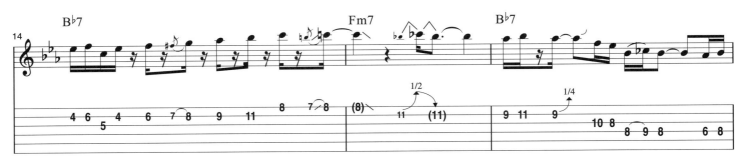

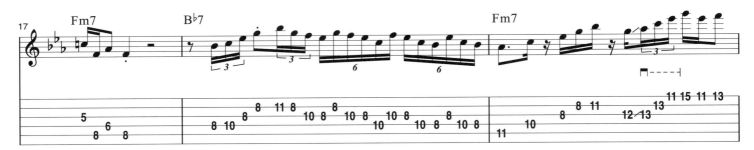

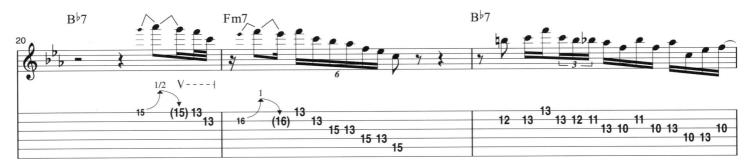

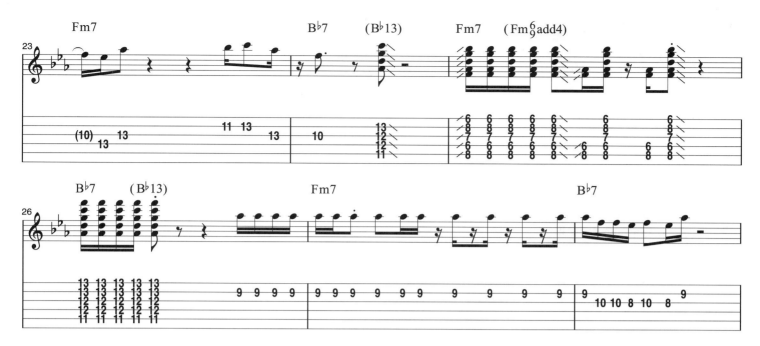

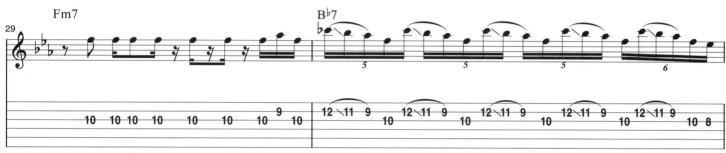

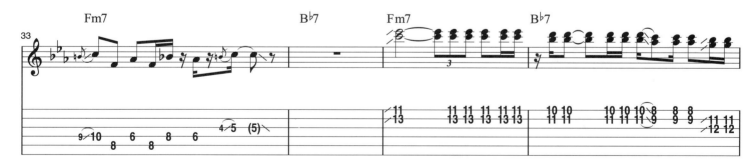

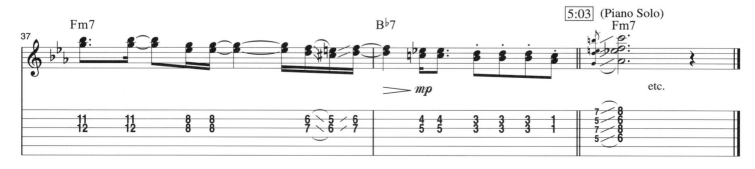

AFFIRMATION
(Breezin')

By Jose Feliciano

Fig.14—Intro

Jose Feliciano's Latin-tinged composition was a highlight of the *Breezin'* sessions and provided an ideal vehicle for the multifarious Benson guitar style. At various points in the tune, he plays exquisite rubato passages, negotiates over changes with a sophisticated bop conception, or decorates a rock groove with funk and blues licks. The 35-second intro is noteworthy. This section is a theme statement in free time and alternates between two minor chords: Em9 and Bm7(sus4). Benson begins unaccompanied and is joined by lush string orchestration midway. Around the two chords, he adds quick ascending runs and tasteful embellishments to the melody. The opening scalar lines in measures 1 and 5 indicate E Dorian (E–F#–G–A–B–C#–D). The fluid rising line in measure 8 is a signature Benson run using a partial Bm9 arpeggio spanning three octaves. The latter is facilitated by his flawless position shifting and strategic string skips. All in all, this is a brief but unforgettable George Benson moment.

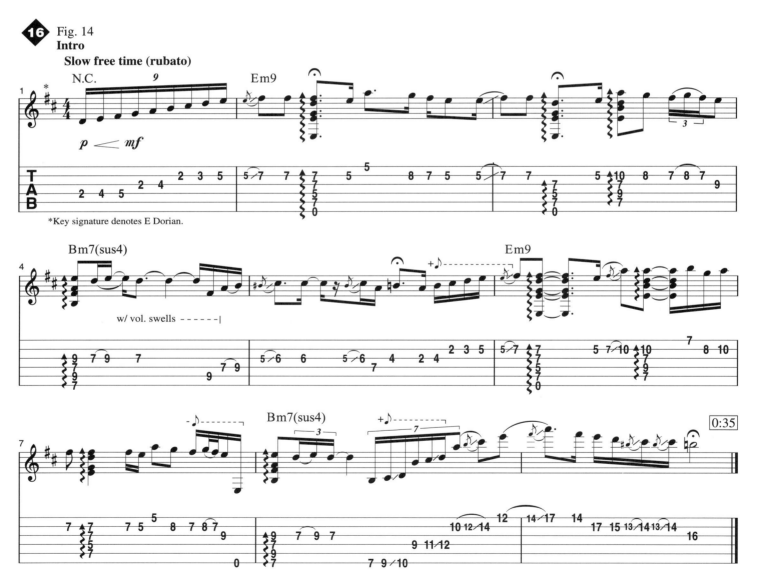

Fig.15—Solo and Interlude

Benson's improvisations in "Affirmation," begun at 2:24, grow organically out of the melody. His playing in the body of the solo is constituted mainly of single notes and employs a patented mix of bop lines, modal jazz melodies, blues-funk licks, and dyad textures. Notice the bop-oriented substitution found in measure 1. Here, he superimposes a familiar Fm9 arpeggio motif on beat 4 over Bm7 to create the sound of an E7#5♭9 altered dominant-seventh chord progressing to Am7 in the next measure. Benson utilizes other characteristic bop elements in measures 2 (beats 3–4), 5, and 17–18. He uses modal sounds in the phrases of measures 3, 9–12, and 25–30. Benson's blues and funk inclinations are at the forefront in measures 13–14, 21–24, and 31–32.

Unmistakable virtuosic flourishes decorate the solo in measures 7, 16, and 29–30. Benson plays a unique and absolutely uncategorizable lick in measure 8. At once chromatic and intervallic, this is a slurred cascade of notes revolving around a high B pedal tone, articulated with Benson's slippery legato technique and lightning-quick picking. Another uncommon Benson lick is found in measures 23-24. This is a *measured trill* played by fretting without picking, using left-hand hammer-on articulation. The trill is based on a D chord and begins with a rapid reiteration of D and A (the tonic and fifth notes of a D chord). Benson often plays these patterns with the first and third fingers at the same fret, but on different strings, to maintain greatest separation of the individual notes and to use the strongest digits for hammering. The phrase concludes with a descending line: A–A♭–G–F#, also played in a similar fashion as a measured trill, in which the lower notes move down chromatically against the stationary higher D pedal tone. This lick is derived from saxophone playing of the post hard-bop genre and is one of several ear-catching horn clichés Benson transferred to the guitar.

The interlude is played in the contrasting tonal center of D (Mixolydian) and finds Benson playing terse rhythmic licks over a funky, rock-inspired ostinato. Note the use of trademark three-note chord shapes in measures 35–38. These shapes are generally voiced as octaves with an inner 4th or 5th tone and are a fixture of Benson's style in both theme statement and improvisational settings.

17 Fig. 15
Guitar Solo
[2:24] **Medium Latin Funk** ♩ = 104

*Signature licks audio fades in 8 measures earlier.

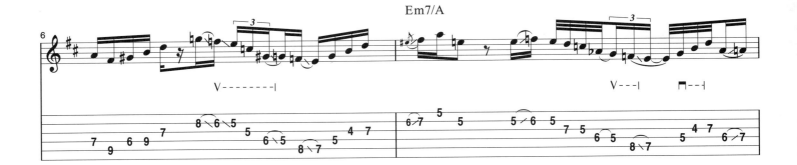

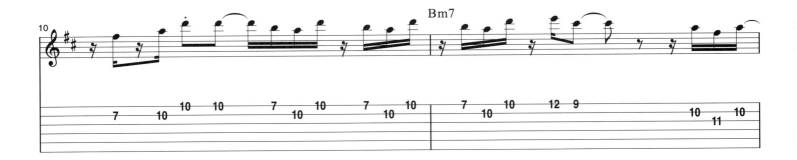

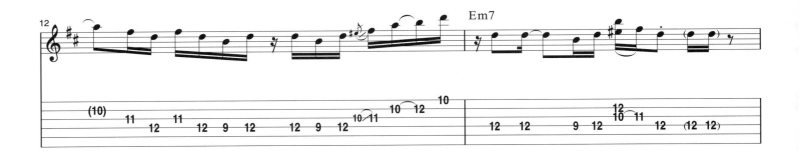

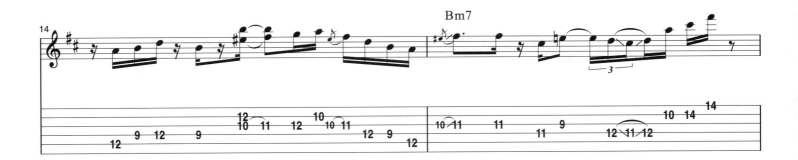

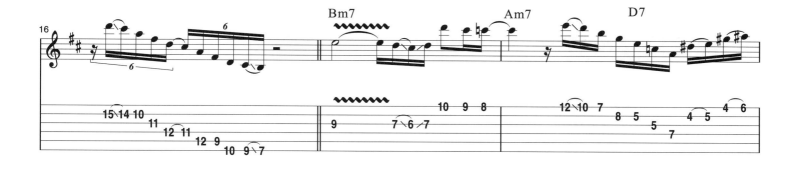

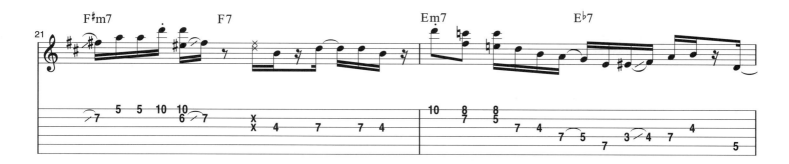

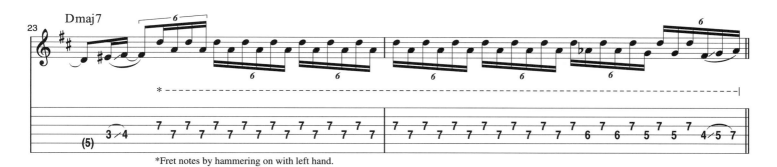

*Fret notes by hammering on with left hand.

3:36 **Interlude**

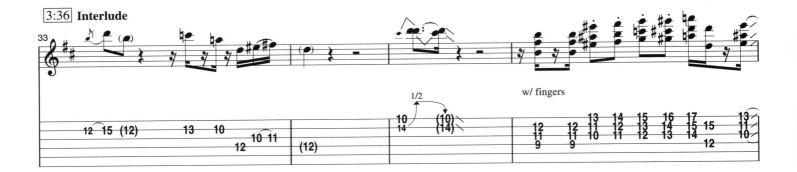

3:50

etc.

C-SMOOTH
(Standing Together, 1998)

By DeChown Jenkins and Jaz Sawyer

Fig.16—Head and Solo

George Benson's collaboration with MDRC yielded this modern R&B-jazz number for his 1998 GRP release *Standing Together*. "C-Smooth" placed Benson's unmistakable guitar voice in yet another contemporary setting, providing further testimony of his ever-broadening musical palette and the continued relevance of his style. As has been his recording practice through the 1990s, he played a variety of archtop electric guitars from his collection into Polytone and Fender amps on the sessions.

"C-Smooth" is a blues in A minor animated by a sultry, slow hip-hop groove, somewhat like a half-time swing feel. An underlying swing rhythm pervades the tune and lends a soulful, elastic quality to Benson's lines. Pronounced blues elements are implicit in the vocalesque pentatonic melody (check out Benson's sweet vibrato in measures 3–4 and 7–8), the call-and-response phrase structure of the head, and the song's 12-bar form. Altered chords are thoughtfully used in the V–IV part of the progression, as in measures 11–12, to expand the tonality beyond traditional blues harmony. Benson gathers momentum during the twenty-four-bar head, adding slinky pentatonic-blues fills in measures 13–14, 17–18, 21–22, and 25–26.

Benson's two-chorus solo contains numerous noteworthy lines. Played exclusively in single notes, his melodies are largely based on the A blues scale (A–C–D–E♭–E–G). They exploit idiomatic blues guitar embellishments such as slides, hammer-ons, pull-offs, string bends, and stylistic vibrato. Characteristic modal lines are found in measures 30–31 and 41–43. These generally lead into and emphasize the modality of the iv chord (Dm). Benson plays bop-based lines in measures 36–38 and 48–51. Note the use of elements such as extended seventh and ninth chord arpeggios, generous chromaticism, and several variants of a familiar Bird-inspired motive in measures 48 (beat 4), 49 (beat 2), and 50 (beats 2–3). The latter occurs within a swirling cascade of notes that caps the solo.

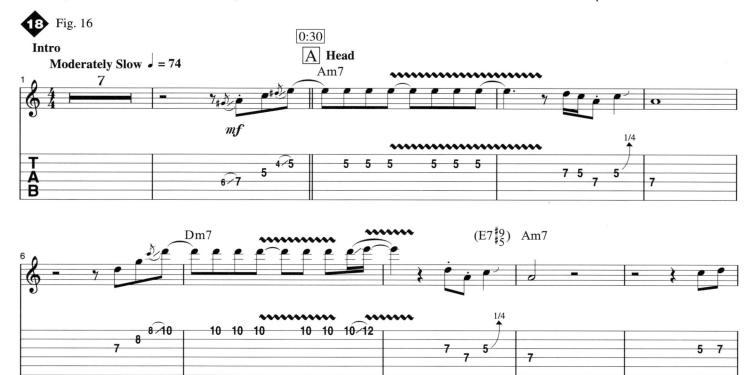

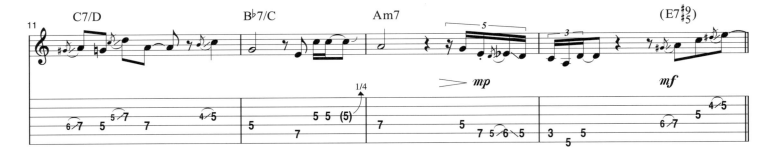

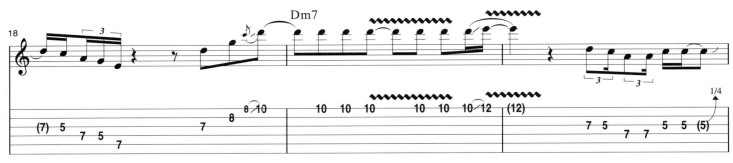

1:49 B Solo: First Chorus

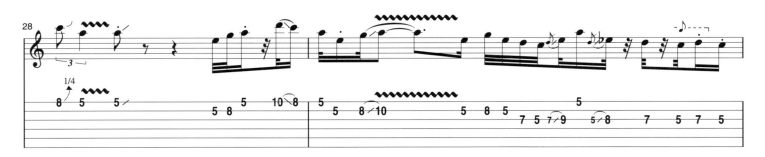

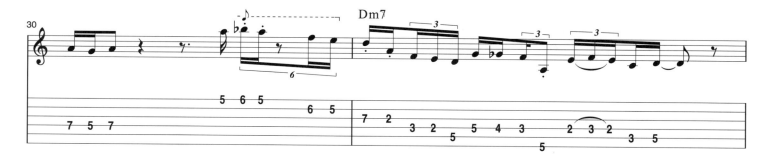

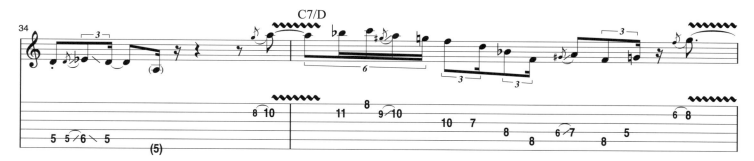

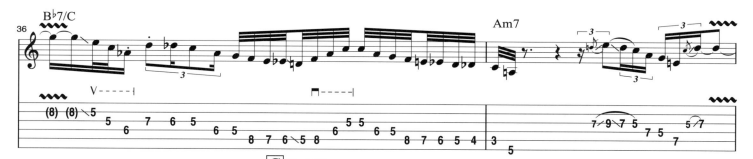

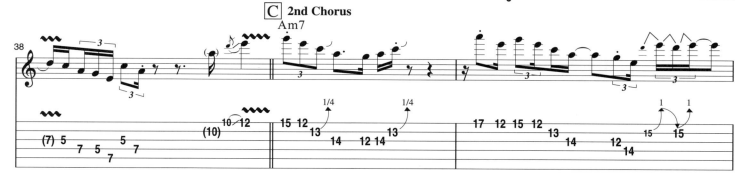

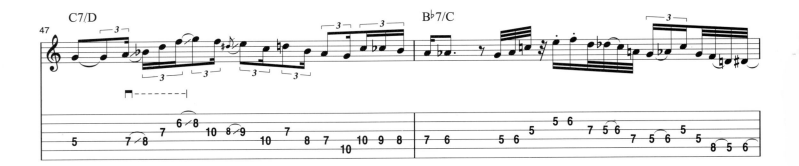

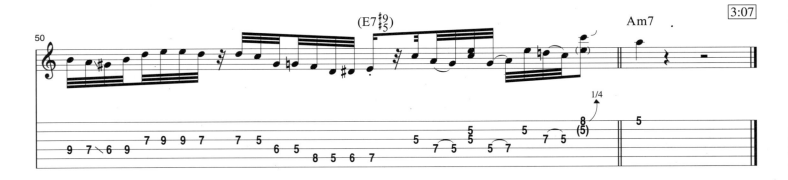